The Scarlet Letter

A guide to Nathaniel Hawthorne's novel
by
Shan Gillard

TABLE OF CONTENTS

AUTHOR BIOGRAPHY

Nathaniel Hawthorne was born on July 4, 1804 in Salem, Massachusetts, to a Puritan family that dated back to the founding of the Massachusetts Bay Colony in 1630. William Hathorne accompanied Governor John Winthrop from England, and became famous as a persecutor of Quakers in Salem. His son, John Hathorne, presided at the Salem Witch trials, and Nathaniel added the "w" to his name in order to distance himself from this ancestor.

After John Hathorne, the family became mariners, and Nathaniel's father was a sea captain who died in 1808 when Nathaniel was four. He grew up in seclusion with his mother, Elizabeth and his two sisters. He and his mother relied on each other for emotional support until the end of her life. An injury to his foot when he was nine required a long period of convalescence, further isolating young Nathaniel and allowing him to absorb an impressive collection of great literature.

Hawthorne left Salem to attend Bowdoin College in Maine in 1821, graduating in 1824. Among his classmates were Henry Wadsworth Longfellow and Franklin Pierce, who became the fourteenth president of the United States. The three became lifelong friends.

After graduation, Hawthorne returned to Salem, working as a writer and contributor to periodicals. His first novel, Fanshawe, was published at his own expense in 1828. Several of his short stories were published in *Twice-Told Tales* in 1837. This was not a financial success, but did establish Hawthorne as a leading writer.

Unable to support himself on what he was earning as a writer, Hawthorne accepted a job as a weigher in the Boston, MS customhouse. Two years later he wrote a series of sketches of New England history for children, *Grandfather's Chair: A History for Youth* (1841), *Famous Old People* (1841), *Liberty Tree* (1841), and *Biographical Stories for Children* (1842). In 1841, Hawthorne also joined Brook Farm, a communal society of intellectuals, hoping that this would give him more time to work on his writing. However, he found the demands of the farm too much, and left after a year.

In 1842 Hawthorne married Sophia Amelia Peabody of Salem, an active participant in the Transcendentalist movement. They lived in Concord until 1846. Hawthorne was unable to make a living as a writer, and growing debts forced him into government service in Salem as surveyor of the Port of Salem. Due to the spoils system, he lost his job in 1849 when there was a change in administration. However, he had already begun writing *The Scarlet Letter*, and this novel was published in 1850, meeting with critical and popular acclaim. It stands as a classic in American literature, and Hawthorne's greatest masterpiece.

Hawthorne moved to Lenox, Massachusetts, where he became friends with Herman Melville, and it was here that he wrote *The House of Seven Gables*, which solidified his success as a literary master. This novel was based on a curse that had been placed on his family during the Salem witch trials. In 1852 he published *The Blithedale Romance*, which deals with the flaws in utopianism.

In 1852 Hawthorne moved back to Concord, writing a campaign biography for his old friend Franklin Pierce. Pierce rewarded Hawthorne by appointing him as consul in Liverpool, England, where he stayed until 1857. The following year was spent in Italy gathering material for his novel *The Marble Faun*, which was published in 1860, and is the story about the conflict between innocence and guilt.

Hawthorne returned to the United States in 1860, just as the Civil War was beginning. His health was poor, and he did not write another novel. He did publish a book of essays, *Our Old Home*, in 1863. He traveled to the mountains in May of 1864 with his friend Franklin Pierce, and died in his sleep on May 19.

Although Hawthorne was not a Christian, his writing was obsessed with the consequences of sin. He was one of the first American writers to explore the emotions and motivations of his characters.

CHAPTERS 1-3

Chapter one simply describes the somber scene of the prison in early 18th century Boston. There is a crowd gathered about this dark and sinister doorway, giving an air of anticipation. Just as Hawthorne is about to leave the scene, he lingers on a solitary rosebush, symbolic of love and hope in this otherwise hopeless panorama. As the matrons of the city stand around gossiping, remonstrating with each other over the leniency of a sentence given and received, the subject of their conjecture is quickly apparent. The prison door opens, and a beautiful young woman exits, with a three month old baby in her arms, and a fantastic scarlet A embroidered on the bust of her dress. The baby has obviously not previously been exposed to the light of day, and blinks at the unaccustomed light. The woman is led to the pillory, where she stands with her child. The woman, Hester Prynne, has committed adultery, and it has been decided that, rather than giving her the usual death penalty, she will be made to stand for three hours on the scaffold, and afterward will be required to wear the scarlet letter for the rest of her life. As she stands on the scaffold, Hester thinks about her childhood, removing herself mentally and insulating herself from the insults and judgmental attitudes of her neighbors. She displays an air of almost haughty defiance, refusing to crumble under their scrutiny.

However, as she surveys the crowd, she suddenly spies a figure on the edge of the crowd, a small, hump-shouldered man who is accompanied by an Indian, and she is obviously disturbed. Their eyes meet, and he raises his finger to his lips, indicating that she should remain silent. The man asks someone in the crowd what is happening, and is told the story — how Hester was sent ahead to Boston by her husband, who has not been heard from in two years. It is believed that her husband has been lost at sea. Because Hester is a beautiful young woman, her sin is considered inevitable, and she has been given a lighter than usual sentence. However, she has not revealed the father of the child. The stranger states that this irks him, and states, "But he will be known! He will be known! He will be known!" Sitting with the governor of the colony is Rev. John Wilson, an elder clergyman of the colony. He speaks to Hester and tries to persuade her to reveal the father's name. Next he appeals to Arthur Dimmesdale, Hester's pastor, to try and convince her that revealing the father's name and repenting will allow her to remove the scarlet letter. She still refuses. Dimmesdale, a young man with a constant nervous tremor, finds her strength and resolve to be "wondrous." By this time her three hours has ended, the child is screaming, and Hester is led back into the darkness of the prison interior.

SUGGESTED ACTIVITIES CHAPTERS 1-3

1.   Draw a picture of the prison, showing the building, the scaffold and the rosebush.

2.   Conduct research into the history of the period. Hawthorne uses the death of Gov. Winthrop, which occurred in 1649, as an event which happens when Pearl is seven. Therefore, the story takes place from 1642-1649. What did Boston look like during those years? How large was it? How did people make their living? How did the laws of the Puritans in Massachusetts differ from those of the rest of the colonies?

3.   Have a discussion about some of the sins represented in the first couple of chapters. Hester had to wear a Scarlet A to represent her "besetting sin" what about some of the other characters that have been introduced, like the women gossiping ? What letter should they be wearing?

4.   Having a child out of wedlock no longer carries the stigma it did at the time of this story. Single parenthood is still not an easy position, especially for young teens. Have students collect formula, diapers, etc. to donate to a shelter for teen moms.

VOCABULARY CHAPTERS 1-3

throng:	a multitude of people crowded together
edifice:	a building
Utopia :	an ideal place or state
virtue:	moral excellence
invariably:	without changing
sepulchers:	a tomb, grave, or burial place
beetle-browed:	having prominent brows
ponderous:	of great weight; heavy; massive
inauspicious:	unfavorable
physiognomies:	faces
augured:	to divine or predict
betokened:	signified by some visible object
tribunal:	a court of justice
vagrant:	an idle person without visible means of support
magistrate:	a civil officer charged with the administration of the law
demeanor:	conduct; behavior; deportment; facial appearance
venerable:	worthy of respect or reverence
transgressor:	one who violates a law; a sinner
scaffold:	any raised platform or stage
infamy:	extremely bad reputation, public reproach, or strong condemnation as a result of a shameful, criminal or outrageous act
impropriety:	the quality or condition of being improper
farthingale:	a hoop petticoat; or circles of hoops, formed of whalebone, used to extend the petticoat
rotundity:	full toned or sonorous
purport:	a purpose or intention
malefactress:	female person who violates the law
hussy:	a brazen or disreputable woman
trow:	to believe, trust, think or suppose
beadle:	a messenger or crier of a court
abashed:	make embarrassed or ashamed
flourishes:	decorations or embellishments
sumptuary:	intended to regulate personal habits on moral or religious grounds
evanescent:	disappearing gradually; fading away
ignominy:	personal disgrace; dishonor
brazen:	boldly shameless
haughty:	disdainfully proud; snobbish; arrogant
rankles:	to continue to irritate or cause bitter resentment
deportment:	conduct; behavior
pillory:	a wooden framework erected on a post, with holes for securing the head and hands, formerly used to expose an offender to public derision
Papist:	a Roman Catholic; one who adheres to the church of Rome and

	the authority of the Pope
mien:	air, being or demeanor
venomous:	spiteful; malignant
preternaturally:	existing or occurring out of the ordinary course of nature; exceptional or abnormal
reminiscences:	mental impressions retained and revived
phantasmagoric:	optical illusions in which figures increase or diminish in size, pass into each other, dissolve, etc.
eminence:	high station, rank, or repute
remonstrance:	an act or instance or protesting, objecting, or complaining
wont:	accustomed to; used to
visage:	the face, usually with reference to shape, features, expression
optics:	eyes
furrowed:	to make wrinkles in the face
heterogeneous:	composed of parts of different kinds
intervolutions:	involving one within another
imperceptible:	very slight or subtle
subsided:	to become quiet, less active
sojourn:	a temporary stay
appended:	added as a supplement
halberds:	a shafted weapon with an axlike cutting blade, beak, and spike
sagacity:	having or showing acute mental discernment; shrewd
obstinacy:	stubbornness
eloquence:	skilled in fluent, forceful and appropriate speech
aspect:	appearance to the eye or mind
impending:	to threaten; menace
melancholy:	a gloomy state of mind
tremulous:	characterized by trembling, as from fear, nervousness, or weakness
impracticable:	not practicable
discourse:	a formal discussion of a subject in speech or written talk, as a sermon
infernal:	hellish; diabolical; fiendish
indifference:	lack of interest or concern
insensibility:	without or not subject to a particular feeling or sensation
remorselessly:	without regret for wrongdoing

QUESTIONS CHAPTERS 1-3

1. What is the symbol that Hawthorne uses for love and hope?

2. What three institutions does Hawthorne say are necessary due to human nature?   Use Rom. 10:13-14; Rom. 5:12; Rom. 6:23; and Rom. 1:28-32 to show why this is true.

3. What is the tone of the story? How does Hawthorne set the tone?

4. Which character is considered to be a witch and will be hanged in the future because   of that identification?

5. The protagonist of the story, who is brought out of the prison door to stand on the   scaffold, is named what? How old is her child?

6. What is the normal punishment for adultery at that time? What is the punishment Hester has received? What has Hester done to embellish the letter? What does this   say about her character?

7. Describe Hester's physical appearance.

8. What representative of the civil government is present as she stands on the scaffold?

9. How does Hester endure her time on the scaffold?

10. As she looks over the people gathered, what does she see?

11. What response does the man have when he sees that she has recognized him?

12. How long has Hester lived in Boston? Where has her husband been?

13. Why has she not been given the usual penalty for adultery?

14. How long does she have to stand on the scaffold?

15. Who is the elder clergyman who speaks to her?

16. Who is Rev. Dimmesdale?

17. Compare and contrast the two clergymen.

18. How is Hester told she could save her soul?

19. Does this meet with what the Bible says about salvation? Give Scripture to support your answer.

20. What is Hester's response? According to Rev. Dimmesdale, what admirable trait is shown by her response?

21. What is the attitude Hester adopts in order to protect herself from the shame she is forced to endure?

22. The setting for *The Scarlet Letter* is in what New England city? What is the century?

23. Imagery is the use of words which appeal to our senses. Find an example of imagery in the first three chapters.

24. A simile is a type of figurative language in which a comparison is made between two objects using like or as. Find an example of a simile.

25. A metaphor is a type of figurative language in which a comparison is made between two objects without using like or as. Find an example of a metaphor.

ANSWERS TO QUESTIONS CHAPTERS 1-3

1.   The rose

2.   The church, cemetery and prison. Rom. 10:13-14 says, "whoever calls on the name of the Lord will be saved. How then shall they call upon Him in whom they have not believed? And how shall they believe in Him whom they have not heard? And how shall they hear without a preacher?" This indicates the necessity for a church to preach the Gospel to those who need to know about salvation. Rom. 5:12 says, "Therefore, just as through one man sin entered into the world, and death through sin, and so death spread to all men, because all sinned – " Rom. 6:23 says, "The wages of sin is death, but the gift of God is eternal life." These verses indicate the need for a cemetery. Rom. 1:28-32 says. "And just as they did not see fit to acknowledge God any longer, God gave them over to a depraved mind, to do those things which are not proper, being filled with all unrighteousness, wickedness, greed, evil; full of envy, murder, strife, deceit, malice, they are gossips, slanderers, haters of God, insolent, arrogant, boastful, inventors of evil, disobedient to parents, without understanding, untrustworthy, unloving, unmerciful, and, although they know the ordinance of God, that those who practice such things are worthy of death, they not only do the same, but also give hearty approval to those who practice them." This would indicate the need for prisons.

3.   The tone of the story is sad and gloomy. Hawthorne accomplishes this through the use of the dark, gloomy setting: the old, dark, weather-stained jail, the old church, the "bettle-browed, gloomy front" of the church, which was the cemetery.

4.   Mistress Hibbins, the governor's sister, was considered to be a witch.

5.   The protagonist is Hester Prynne, and her daughter is three months old.

6.   The normal punishment for adultery is death, but Hester has to wear a scarlet A for the rest of her life. Hester has embellished the letter with a flourish of gold thread, indicating that she is an individualist, and is not willing to submit to the ruling of the magistrates without making some personal protest.

7.   Hester was very tall, with an elegant figure, thick, dark, glossy hair that gleams in the sunshine; a beautiful complexion, dark brow and dark eyes. She is very graceful and dignified.

8. Governor Bellingham

9. Hester brings up memories from her childhood, rather than dwell on the people who are gawking at her from the audience gathered around the scaffold.

10. She sees an old man, on the edge of the crowd, standing with an Indian. The man is dressed in a rather strange manner and is a stranger in town. One of his shoulders is higher than the other, and his description corresponds to one of her memories from her past.

11. He lays his finger on his lips, indicating that she should remain silent, not giving away her recognition of him.

12. Hester has been in Boston for two years. Her husband had sent her on ahead of him, while he stayed in Europe to settle his business matters. It is believed that he has drowned on the passage from Europe.

13. Because Hester is young and exceptionally beautiful, it is believed that she cannot be held entirely responsible for her fall into temptation.

14. three hours.

15. John Wilson

16. Rev. Dimmesdale is Hester Prynne's pastor

17. Both Rev. Dimmesdale and Wilson are scholarly and intellectual, men who are held in high esteem by their communities as godly leaders. Rev. Wilson is the eldest clergyman in the colony, described as having "gizzled locks" and a kindly manner, although he has spent more time developing his studious side than his pastoral, kindly side. When he deals with Hester, he defers to Rev. Dimmesdale, nevertheless chastising him for being "oversoft." Rev. Dimmesdale is very young, unsure of himself, uncomfortable with the public attention and perpetually displaying a frightened, anxious demeanor.

18. Rev. Wilson tells her to repent and reveal the name of the baby's father.

19. This view of salvation does not correspond with the biblical view of salvation as a free gift of God. The salvation offered to Hester is a salvation of works. Rom. 6:23 says, "the wages of sin is death, but the gift of God is eternal life." Eph. 2:8-9 says, "For by grace you have

been saved through faith; and that not of yourselves, it is the give of God; not as a result of works that no one should boast." This is exactly the opposite of what was offered to Hester.

20. Hester refuses to reveal the father's name: "I will not speak," she says that her child will have to know a heavenly Father, because "she shall never know an earthly one!" Rev. Dimmesdale feels she should be admired for her strength and generosity.

21. Hester adopts an attitude of indifference, verging on haughtiness.

22. *The Scarlet Letter* is set in Boston, MS in the 17th century (1642-1649).

23. Examples of imagery: "A throng of bearded men, in sad-colored garments and gray, steepled-crowned hats;" "heavily timbered with oak and studded with iron spikes;" "beetle-browed and gloomy front;" "a wild rose-bush, covered, in this month of June, with its delicate gems, which might be imagined to offer their fragrance and fragile beauty to the prisoner."

24. Examples of similes: "like a black shadow emerging into the sunshine;" "as if her heart had been flung into the street for them all to spurn and trample upon;" "like a mass of imperfectly shaped and spectral images;" "like a tuft of green moss on a crumbling wall;" "like a man chiefly accustomed to look inward;" "like a snake gliding swiftly over them;" "like the darkly engraved portraits which we see prefixed to old volumes of sermons;" "as of a being who felt himself quite astray and at a loss in the pathway of human existence;" "pale as death."

25. **Examples of metaphors: "the black flower of civilized society;" "the naughty baggage;" "the** image of Divine Maternity;" "that sacred image of sinless motherhood;" "the entire track along which she had been treading since her happy infancy;" "The Daniel who shall expound it is yet a-wanting;" "She will be a living sermon against sin."

CHAPTERS 4-6

As Hester and her child return to the prison, the agitation of the mother and child lead the jailer to call for the services of a physician, the same stranger noticed in the previous encounter with Hester. The man has been housed in the jail while the town officials have been arranging for a ransom to have him returned from his captivity with the Indians. The man is using the name Roger Chillingworth, but it becomes immediately apparent that he is Dr. Prynne, Hester's husband. After Chillingworth mixes medicine for the baby, but Hester refuses to administer it to the child, afraid that he might be trying to poison her. He tells her that he does not want to harm the child, proceeding to administer the medicine to her himself. The child is soon quiet, and he concocts another mixture for Hester. Again, she fears he might be trying to give her something to harm her, but he says he prefers to allow the shame of the scarlet letter to have its effect in her life. He goes on to confess that he has wronged her because he should not have expected someone as young as she to have been married to an old man such as he. In this way he has contributed to her sinful state. He tells her that, since he has wronged her and she has wronged him, they are even, but the man who is the father of the child has wronged them both; it is her duty to reveal the man to Chillingworth. When Hester refuses, he tells her that he has ways of knowing what is going on in a person's heart, and he will know the man when he "trembles" and "shudders." Chillingworth further swears Hester to secrecy concerning their relationship, preferring to allow the citizens of Boston to continue to believe he has drowned than to know he is the husband of one who is shamed.

After Hester is released from prison, she takes up residence in a remote cottage and makes her living by sewing – the scarlet letter has become an advertisement of her ability with the needle. She is called upon to make all manner of garments for special occasions, with the exception of a wedding veil, which she is never allowed to make. She is shunned by all of her neighbors, and lives a lonely existence with only her child for a companion. Although she always dresses herself in plain attire (except for her scarlet A) the clothing she makes for her child is elaborate and colorful. Any extra income that she has is given to feed and clothe the poor, but she is treated as badly by them as by the more prominent citizens of the community. As Hester goes about her business in the town, she often finds herself the subject of impromptu sermons, and even the children scream at her. She begins to believe she has some special sensitivity to the sins of others around her.

Hester has named her child Pearl – because she is her mother's only treasure, bought with a great price. Pearl is a precocious child, beautiful, intelligent, and wild. She loves the sunshine and is difficult to control. Hester finds it nearly impossible to discipline her. Pearl has no playmates – the children treat her with the same aversion as her mother is treated by their parents. Rather than creating imaginary friends, Pearl creates imaginary enemies of sticks, pretending they are the Puritan children, and then destroying them. The only time Hester is truly at peace with her daughter is when Pearl sleeps, and she sometimes fears that Pearl is not truly human, but partly demonic. In addition, Pearl's first smile comes, not in response to her mother's face, but in response to the scarlet letter, adding to Hester's grief.

SUGGESTED ACTIVITIES: CHAPTERS 4-6

1. Pearl is a lonely child, ostracized by society. There are many children in need today. Challenge your students to adopt a child through Compassion, International or Feed the Children, etc.

2. Have students undertake embroidery projects that can be presented as gifts to residents of a local nursing home.

VOCABULARY CHAPTERS 4-6

perpetrate:	to carry out; enact; commit
quell:	to suppress; subdue; crush
singular:	unusual or strange
sagamores:	among some tribes of American Indians, a king or chief
amenable:	willing to yield; agreeable
intimated:	hint; imply; suggest
peremptory:	leaving no opportunity for denial or refusal
alchemy:	a form of chemistry and speculative philosophy of the Middle Ages that attempted to discover an elixir of life
draught:	the quantity of liquor drank at once
misbegotten:	illegitimate
efficacy:	capacity for producing a desired result; effectiveness
leech:	(obsolete) a physician; a professor of the art of healing
Lethe:	oblivion
Nepenthe:	a drug of medicine that drives away pain and grief
requital:	an action in return for service, kindness, etc.
Paracelsus:	A Swiss physician who lived at the close of the 15th century
quaff:	drink with hearty enjoyment
expostulation:	reasoning with someone by way of warning or rebuke
feigned:	represent fictitiously; pretend
epoch:	a period of time marked by distinctive features
sombre:	gloomy; dark; shadowy
wrought:	worked
retribution:	requital according to merits or deserts, esp. for evil
enjoin:	to prohibit or restrain
paramour:	an illicit lover
wottest:	to know; be aware of
morbid:	suggesting an unhealthy mental state or attitude; gloomy
lurid:	gruesome; horrible; revolting
sufficed:	to be enough or adequate
assimilate:	to take in and incorporate as one's own; absorb
galling:	to make sore by rubbing; chafe
fain:	gladly; willingly
sable:	black; dark
progenitors:	a person or thing that originates something or serves as a

model
plebeian: of or pertaining to the common people
emolument: compensation, as fees or tips, from employment
commiseration: the action of feeling or expressing sympathy for
pomp: stately or splendid display; splendor
ruff: a neckpiece of lace gathered into deep, full, regular folds
ascetic: austere; simple
superfluous: being more than is sufficient or required; excessive
penance: a punishment undergone as penitence for sin
voluptuous: characterized by or ministering to indulgence in luxury
succor: to help or relieve in difficulty, need or distress
imbibed: to receive into the mind
insidious: intended to entrap or beguile
guise: general external appearance
contumaciously: stubbornly perverse or rebellious; willfully disobedient
sullied: soiled; tarnished; stained
talisman: good luck charm
vulgar: common people of society
averred: to assert or affirm with confidence
incredulity: the quality of being unable to believe
inscrutable: not easily understood; mysterious
procured: to obtain
imbued: to saturate deeply
mutability: subject to change or alteration
prolific: highly productive
caprice: a sudden unpredictable change
sprite: an elf, fairy or goblin
intangibility: not material
placidity: peacefulness
disporting: displaying in a sporting manner
scourging: whip or lash, esp. for punishment
anathemas: curses
reviled: to speak abusively
ejaculation: an abrupt, exclamatory utterance
gesticulation: the act of using gestures in an excited manner
query: a question; an inquiry
labyrinth: a maze

QUESTIONS CHAPTERS 4-6

1. As Hester returns to prison, what is her state of mind? How does this affect her child?

2. Who does the jailer bring in for assistance? What is the name the man is using? Who is he really?

3. Why does Hester hesitate to give the child the medicine?

4. Why does he tell Hester he has wronged her?

5. For what reason does he say that she should reveal the child's father to him? How does he say he will know the man?

6. What promise does he extract from Hester concerning their relationship? What biblical principles is he causing her to violate?

7. What are the three reasons Hester decides to stay in Boston, rather than returning to England or going to some other place where she will not be known?

8. Besides being a symbol of her shame, how does the scarlet letter become helpful to Hester in making her living?

9. What kinds of things does Hester make? What is she not allowed to make?

10. What does Hester do with any money she has above what she needs to pay for the needs of herself and her child?

11. How are her efforts received?

12. How is Hester treated by the people of the community?

13. What does the passage mean, "she felt an eye – a human eye – upon the ignominious brand, that seemed to give a momentary relief, as if half of her agony were shared. The next instant, back it all rushed again, with still a deeper throb of pain; for, in that brief interval, she had sinned anew. Had Hester sinned alone?"?

14. Hester's imagination leads her to believe that the scarlet letter allows her to discern what about other people?

15. What is the name Hester gave to her child? Why?

16. How does Hester's treatment of her child correspond with Prov. 3:11-12; 13:24; 19:18; 22:15; 23:13-14?

17. How does Hester dress her child?

18. Describe the child.

19. How do the other children of the town treat Hester's child?

20. How does the child play?

21. What is the only time when Hester can take comfort in her child?

22. What does Hester question about the child?

23. What is the child's response when Hester tells her she has been sent from the Heavenly Father?

24. What is the first thing the child notices about Hester?

25. What do the people of Boston believe about the child?

ANSWERS TO QUESTIONS CHAPTERS 4-6

1. Hester iss extremely agitated, and it is affecting her child to the point the infant will not stop crying.

2. The jailer brings the stranger who has been recognized by Hester, because he is a physician. He is using the name Roger Chillingworth, but he is actually Dr. Prynne, Hester's husband.

3. She is afraid he is trying to poison the child.

4. He is much older than she, and has dedicated his life to scholarship. He should have known that an older man such as he could not expect a young, vibrant woman to remain faithful to him. He wronged her by placing her in a cold, loveless marriage.

5. He tells Hester that their wrongs have balanced each other, but the wrong done by the father of the child was done equally to both of them. For this reason, he feels he deserves to know who the man is. When she refuses to tell him, he tells her he will know the man by his trembling and shuddering.

6. He makes Hester promise not to reveal his identity, but to allow people to continue to believe that her husband has drowned. Prov. 19:9, 25:18, and Matt. 19:18 all speak against being a false witness, and that is what Chillingworth is asking Hester to be.

7. The three reasons Hester stayed in Boster were:
   a. Her sin occurred in Boston and her child was born here, so she feels she has roots there.
   b. Her lover is still there, and she holds out hope that one day they will somehow be able to be together.
   c. She feels she deserves to suffer the punishment for her sin, and somehow that will bring her salvation.

8. Hester makes her living by needlework, so the elaborate needlework surrounding the scarlet letter has become somewhat of an advertisement.

9. She makes all kinds of garments for special occasions, from formal ceremonial garments for the installation of magistrates, to funeral attire, to baby clothing. The only thing Hester was never allowed to make was a bridal veil.

10. Hester provides food and clothing for those who are the poor, who are in worse condition than she is.

11. They repay her by treating her with contempt, ingratitude and insults.

12. The people of the community treat her as an outcast, having nothing to do with her unless a clergyman is in the vicinity and decides to use her as an object lesson for an impromptu sermon when she is out on the street. It becomes so difficult that she prefers to only go out at night.

13. There are times when her lover looks on the scarlet letter, and she feels at that moment that she has a lessening of the burden of guilt, as it is shared by him. However, she is so conditioned to her guilt and her belief that she must suffer this punishment in order to serve penance for her sin, that she immediately feels guilty even for thinking that she can share this burden. Hawthorne asks the question, "Had Hester sinned alone?" Obviously she had not, but her decision to keep the identity of the father secret had led her to feel she must bear the guilt alone.

14. She believes she can discern the sin that is in other people's lives.

15. She names the child Pearl, because she is her only treasure, and was bought with a great price. Pearl is her greatest joy and only companion, and she is also her greatest grief, as she constantly reminds her of the sin that brought her into the world.

16. All of the passages in Proverbs speak of the necessity of disciplining children, but Hester is not able to bring herself to discipline Pearl at all, allowing Pearl's wild nature to be in control of most situations.

17. She dresses Pearl in the most vibrant, gorgeous, luxurious garments she can design and concoct. Pearl is as elaborately dressed as Hester is drably dressed.

18. Pearl is a very intelligent, very pretty child with a vivid imagination and a propensity to be constantly in motion. She is moody and flighty, given to temper tantrums when she does not get her way, and she knows how to play on her mother's emotions.

19. The other children scream when they see Pearl, and have nothing to do with her, picking up on their parents' attitude toward Pearl's mother.

20. Pearl plays with things in nature, to the point that she will set up little twigs and pretend that they are the Puritan elders and their children, then destroys them all.

21. She can only take comfort in Pearl when she is asleep.

22. She questioned whether or not Pearl is really human.

23. "He did not send me! I have no Heavenly Father!"

24. the scarlet letter

25. The people of Boston believed that Pearl is a demonic child.

CHAPTERS 7-8

Hester is on her way to Governor Bellingham's mansion to deliver a pair of gloves she has embroidered, but also to appeal to the governor because she has heard that there are those in the town who have decided that Pearl should be taken from her. As Hester walks along with Pearl trotting beside her, Pearl's attire suggests that she is a human form of the scarlet letter – she is wearing a red dress with gold trim. Some children along the way grasp this very idea, suggesting to one another that they should throw mud on Hester and Pearl. However, Pearl runs at the children, shakes her fist, and screams, sending the children running; returning to Hester with a smile.

When they reach the governor's mansion, they are admitted, but he is with someone, and Hester and Pearl have to wait. Pearl becomes fascinated with a suit of armor in the hall. The reflection of her mother in the concave surface of the helmet causes the scarlet letter to be emphasized, and Pearl standing beside her becomes a second scarlet letter. Hester leads Pearl out to the garden in order to distract her.

The governor enters with the Rev. Wilson, Rev. Dimmesdale and Roger Chillingworth. When he first sees Pearl, he does not know she is Hester's child, and compares her to a bird. After he realizes who she is, Hester comes forward, petitioning him to leave Pearl in her custody and not take her away. At this point, Rev. Wilson begins to question the child to see if she is being taught properly concerning the things of God. Although Pearl, at three, is very precocious and is capable of answering any of his questions, she suddenly becomes capricious and, when asked who made her, she says she was plucked from the rose bush that grew by the prison door. Of course, this merely cements the thoughts of the men that Pearl is not going to receive a proper upbringing with Hester, and they need to take her away and place her with someone else. Hester passionately pleads with them to not take her, then suddenly turns to Dimmesdale and appeals to him to speak for her. Dimmesdale, who has become weaker and more emaciated, as well as developing a habit of keeping his hand over his heart, does plead Hester's case. He theorizes it is possible that leaving Pearl with Hester will keep Hester from falling into greater sin. Chillingworth comments, "You speak, my friend, with a strange earnestness," indicating he has noticed Dimmesdale's interest in the matter may be deeper than just that of a pastor. It is decided that Pearl will be allowed to stay with Hester on the condition that she attend school and church, and Rev. Dimmesdale will be responsible for examining her and making sure she is making appropriate progress. As Hester leaves, Mistress Hibbins invites Hester to the forest with her to meet the Black Man. Hester declines, since she must be at home to take care of Pearl, proving Dimmesdale's argument true.

SUGGESTED ACTIVITIES CHAPTERS 7-8

1. Hawthorne emphasizes the connection between Pearl and the scarlet letter, and constantly describes Pearl as a wild bird. Have students make posters showing what Pearl is like as a three-year-old.

2. Have students research the influence of witchcraft at this period in the history of Boston.

3. Assign students biographies of some of the historical figures represented during this time: Governor Winthrop, the Apostle Eliot, Anne Hutchison, etc.

VOCABULARY CHAPTERS 7-8

impelled:	to drive or urge forward
ludicrous:	causing or deserving laughter because of absurdity; ridiculous
pristine:	having its original purity
intrinsic:	belonging to a thing by its very nature
imperious:	domineering; dictatorial
unpremeditated:	not planned beforehand
wan:	showing or suggesting ill health
pallid:	pale; faint or deficient in color
similitude:	likeness; resemblance
analogy:	a similarity between like features of two things
urchins:	any small boy or youngster
dauntless:	bold; not intimidated
pestilence:	a deadly or virulent epidemic disease
extant:	still existing
cabalistic:	containing an occult meaning
caper:	to leap or skip about in a sprightly manner
flanked:	to occupy a position at the flank or side
portal:	a door, gate or entrance
embowed:	to form like a bow, to arch; to vault
tome:	a book, esp. a very heavy, large, or learned book
cuirass:	a breast-plate; a piece of defensive armor
gorget:	a piece of armor for defending the neck or throat
greaves:	armor for the legs; a sort of boots
gauntlets:	a large iron glove with fingers covered with small plates
burnished:	polished
panoply:	a wide-ranging and impressive array or display
muster:	to assemble troops, as for battle or inspection
exigences:	a state of urgency or emergency
relinquished:	to give up; surrender
eldritch:	weird; eerie
expatiating:	to elaborate in discourse or writing

antiquated:	old fashioned; obsolete
reproof:	criticism or correction
genial:	warmly and pleasantly cheerful
benevolence:	desire to do good to others
physic:	the art or practice of healing medicine
court mask:	masquerade party
apparitions:	ghosts; specters
bedizen:	to dress or adorn gaudily or tastelessly
catechism:	instruction by question and answer
temporal:	of or pertaining to time
proximity:	nearness in place, time, relation, etc.
depravity:	the state of being morally corrupt or evil
indefeasible:	not to be defeated
emaciated:	abnormally thin and wasted away
mountebank:	a charlatan or quack who sells to an audience using tricks
adduced:	to bring forward, as in evidence
vehemence:	impassioned; marked by great energy or vigor
unobtrusive:	not imposing oneself on others
withal:	with it all; as well
sundering:	to separate; part; divide

QUESTIONS CHAPTERS 7-8

1. Where is Hester going? What are her two reasons for going there?

2. Why do the leaders of the town want to do what they are planning?

3. How is Pearl dressed? What does this make her appear to be?

4. What do the children of the town do when they see Pearl? How does Pearl handle   the situation?

5. Compare the way Pearl must feel to the way the psalmist feels in Ps. 31:11 and 142:4.

6. What does the governor's servant think of Hester?

7. What fascinates Pearl in the entryway? How does she use it to distress her mother?

8. When Hester distracts Pearl by taking her into the garden, what symbol does   Hawthorne use again?

9. When Governor Bellingham enters, who accompanies him?

10. Why is Roger Chillingworth there?

11. What explanation is given for Rev. Dimmesdale's failing health?

12. What metaphor does Rev. Wilson use to refer to Pearl when he first sees her?

13. What biblical symbol does Governor Bellingham use in referring to Hester?

14. When Rev. Wilson calls Pearl to him, how does she react to him? What simile does Hawthorne use in referring to her for the second time?

15. When asked who made her, what is Pearl's response?

16. How has Roger Chillingworth changed in the three years since Hester has last seen   him?

17. When Hester is told they will take Pearl from her, to whom does she appeal for a defense?

18. What gesture does Rev. Dimmesdale make when he is very nervous?

19.   According to Rev. Dimmesdale, what eternal benefit will Hester gain by being allowed   to bring up Pearl?

20.   What is wrong with this line of thinking?

21.   What are the three conditions that have to be satisfied for Hester to be allowed to   keep Pearl?

22.   What gesture of affection does Pearl make toward Rev. Dimmesdale?

23.   What does Rev. Wilson say Pearl has in her?

24.   As Hester and Pearl leave, who appears at the window?

25.   How does Hawthorne tie Hester's response to Mrs. Hibbins to Rev. Dimmesdale's argument for Hester?

ANSWERS TO QUESTIONS CHAPTERS 7-8

1. She is going to Governor Bellingham's mansion to deliver some gloves she has embroidered, and to appeal to him because she has heard that there is a movement to remove Pearl from her custody.

2. The rumor that Pearl was a child of demonic origin has made them feel that she is a stumbling block to Hester's soul, and should be removed. If Pearl is not a demon child and holds promise for being a morally upright adult, they need to place her into a more proper environment so that she will be properly taught.

3. Pearl is wearing a red dress with gold trim, making her appear to be a human version of the scarlet letter.

4. The children decide to run beside her and throw mud at her, but Pearl runs at them, shaking her fists and screaming, sending them running away.

5. These verses tell how the psalmist feels that he is an outcast and that no one cares for his soul. Even though Pearl is only a three-year-old, she must feel the same way. No one in the world but her mother cares for her.

6. He thinks she must be a very important person to have such an elaborate symbol on her dress.

7. Pearl is fascinated by the armor, especially by the reflection in the concave mirror of the helmet. This causes distress for Hester, since it emphasizes the scarlet letter and doubles the letter with Pearl standing beside her.

8. The rose

9. Rev. John Wilson, Rev. Arthur Dimmesdale, Roger Chillingworth

10. He is Rev. Dimmesdale's friend and physician.

11. He has sacrificed his health for his pastoral duties.

12. He calls her a "bird of scarlet plumage."

13. He refers to her as a type of Babylon. This symbol is used because the Bible refers to Babylon as a harlot – a reference to it as a false religion.

14. Instead of coming to him like children usually do, she flees from him. Hawthorne says she is "like a wild tropical bird of rich plumage ready to take flight into the upper air."

15. She says she was not made at all, "but plucked by her mother off the bush of wild roses that grew by the prison door."

16. He seems to have become uglier; darker in complexion and more misshapen.

17. Rev. Dimmesdale.

18. He places his hand over his heart.

19. He argues that having the child in her care may keep Hester from becoming involved in something more sinful, and may result in bringing her (Hester) to salvation.

20. This does not correspond with a biblical view of salvation, because it requires Hester to work for her salvation by caring for the child. However, Eph. 2:8-9 says that salvation comes by grace through faith, not by works.

21. Pearl has to attend school, attend church, and be taught in catechism and examined by Rev. Dimmesdale.

22. Pearl caresses his hand with her cheek.

23. witchcraft

24. Mistress Hibbins

25. Hester tells her that if they had taken Pearl from her, she would have accompanied her to the forest to be with the Black Man, but because she has Pearl, she has to stay at home.

CHAPTERS 9-11

When Roger Chillingworth first comes to Boston, he is able to fit right into the fabric of the town, because he brings with him the skills of a physician, and there is no physician in the town. Of course, he is really Roger Prynne, and he had originally come to claim his bride and settle down with her. Finding her in the compromised position of a woman taken in adultery, he chooses instead to secretly disown her and take a new identity for himself. In addition to his formal studies in Europe, he had learned much about herbs from the Indians, and is able to use this knowledge as well. Because of the failing health of Rev. Dimmesdale, Chillingworth immediately attaches himself to the young man. Dimmesdale is a scholar who is believed to have great potential, but his health has begun to fail. Some believe that the world is not worthy of him, but Dimmesdale says that if God removes him from the world, it will be because of his own unworthiness. Chillingworth speaks with intimate knowledge of well known European physicians, and the people of Boston believe that they are indeed blessed to have this man brought to them; some even believe that God plucked him from Europe and dropped him into their midst. As time passes and the relationship between the two men becomes closer, Chillingworth begins to hint that he would better be able to treat Dimmesdale if they lived under the same roof. At the urging of others, this is finally accomplished. They move into a widow's house near the graveyard, and Chillingworth turns his rooms into a study and laboratory. Dimmesdale's room has a sunny exposure, and he has biblical tapestries representing the story of David and Bathsheba and Nathan the Prophet on his walls. These are particularly appropriate, as the story of David and Bathsheba refers to his sin with Hester, and Nathan the Prophet is symbolic of Chillingworth. As Chillingworth's appearance begins to change, the opinions of the people also begin to change. A man who had been in England remembers seeing him there under another name, connected to a murder. Some believe he is a demonic agent, and Dimmesdale has come under the influence of the devil.

As their relationship grows, Chillingworth's fascination with the inner workings of Dimmesdale's heart also grows. He feels that Dimmesdale is hiding something from him, and probes in their conversations. However, Dimmesdale is willing only to discuss philosophy, religion, etc. One day, as Dimmesdale finds Chillingworth examining some ugly plants, he asks him where he found them. Chillingworth tells him he took them from the graveyard, growing from the heart of an unrepentant sinner, hinting to Dimmesdale to confess his sin to Chillingworth. Dimmesdale tells him that, although he knows the joy that comes from the unburdening of a sinful heart, there are some who prefer not to publicly confess in order to be able to better serve others. Chillingworth tells him that these men deceive themselves. At this point, they are interrupted by a child's laughter, and see Pearl dancing on the graves. Hester tries to convince her to behave, but Pearl picks up prickly burrs and arranges them along the scarlet letter. Chillingworth says that, "there is no law, or reverence for authority mixed up in that child's composition." Dimmesdale says, "none- save the freedom of a broken law." Pearl then throws one of the prickly burrs at Dimmesdale, and he shrinks back. Pearl claps her hands, then tells her mother to come away before the Black Man catches her like he has caught the Minister. After they leave, Chillingworth again tries to convince Dimmesdale to confess to him, but he becomes angry and says that he will never confess to an earthly physician. Chillingworth observes that he is capable of passion and has committed some passionate act before. Sometime later, he finds Dimmesdale asleep, moves his clerical garments aside, and sees something on the man's chest that causes him great ecstasy.

Now convinced that Dimmesdale is his man, Chillingworth decides that he will attach himself closer to Dimmesdale than ever. Although Dimmesdale suspects something, he chastises himself for having such thoughts about a man who is only trying to help him, and pushes them to the back of his mind. As Dimmesdale's bodily strength fails, his popularity and reputation grow stronger. His agony over his own sin helps him to be sensitive to the needs and suffering of his congregation, and people admire him and hold him up as a holy and godly man. Feeling that he should be punished even as Hester is punished, he takes it upon himself to punish himself in private. He keeps a scourge in his closet and scourges himself; he keeps long fasts until he is so weak he is trembling; he sits in the dark and then stares into a mirror in the light, contemplating his sin. Throughout all of this, he sees visions of demons, angels, dead friends, his parents, Hester and Pearl.

VOCABULARY CHAPTERS 9-11

appellation:	name
vindicate:	to clear, as from an accusation or suspicion
chirurgical:	surgical
apothecary:	a druggist
pharmacopoeia:	a book containing a list of drugs
scrupulous:	rigorously precise or correct
vigils:	a period of watchful attention maintained at night or other times
nether:	lying or believed to lie beneath the earth's surface; infernal
interposition:	the act of placing between
importunate:	begging earnestly
orthodox:	conforming to the approved form of any doctrine
scrutinized:	to examine minutely
concord:	agreement between things; harmony
erudition:	knowledge acquired by study
vilified:	to speak ill of; defame; slander
decried:	denounce
diabolical:	devilish; fiendish
sexton:	an official who maintains a church building and its contents
stealthily:	secretly or providing the capacity to escape detection
inimical:	unfavorable; harmful
propagate:	to cause an increase in number or amount
burdock:	a coarse broad-leaved weed bearing prickly heads of burs that stick to clothing
perforce:	necessarily
eccentricities:	oddities or peculiarities of conduct
conjoined:	joined together; united
anon:	in a short time; soon
palliate:	to relieve without curing
proffering:	to put before a person for acceptance
somniferous:	causing sleep
vestment:	garments worn by the clergy
hitherto:	up to this time
latent:	present but not visible; dormant
balked:	to stop short and stubbornly refuse to go on
antipathy:	a natural repugnance; aversion
abhorrence:	detestable; loathsome
presentiments:	a feeling that something bad is going to happen
machinations:	a crafty scheme or maneuver; an intrigue
abstruse:	hard to understand
efficacious:	capable of having the desired result or effect
unamiable:	not friendly
etherealized:	to make heavenly or celestial
introspection:	given to examining one's own thoughts and emotions
undissembled:	not giving a false or misleading appearance to

QUESTIONS CHAPTERS 9-11

1. Before Roger Chillingworth came to Boston, who took care of the health needs of the community?

2. How do the people feel about Rev. Dimmesdale and his failing health?

3. When Chillingworth first comes to Boston, what do some people say about his method of being transported there?

4. Whose idea is it for the two men to move into the same home?

5. What is the significance of the tapestries hanging on Rev. Dimmesdale's walls?

6. As time passes, what differences do the people of the town notice about Chillingworth's appearance? What does this lead them to conclude about him?

7. What simile does Hawthorne use to describe the way in which Chillingworth is digging into Dimmesdale's heart?

8. When Dimmesdale asks where he found the strange plant he is studying in his laboratory, what response does Chillingworth give him?

9. Dimmesdale says that some people seem unable to make public professions during their lifetime, but they will confess with a "joy unutterable" at what time?

10. For what reason does Dimmesdale say that it is impossible for some to confess their sins openly during their lifetime (referring to his own sin)?

11. How does Dimmesdale's justification of his inability to confess his sin line up with the Bible in Prov. 28:13; Isa. 29:15; Luke 12:2; 12:8; I John 1:9?

12. What interrupts the conversation the men are having?

13. What does Dimmesdale mean when he says that the only reverence for authority in Pearl is the freedom of a broken law?

14. What insight does Pearl show about the situation that indicates a wisdom beyond her age?

15. When Chillingworth indicates that Dimmesdale should confess what is in his soul in order to cure his physical ailments, what is Dimmesdale's reply?

16. What happens while Dimmesdale is asleep?

17. What plan does Chillnigworth devise in order to carry out his revenge? How has this changed from his original stated intent?

18. How does the minister respond to Chillingworth's influence?

19. How does Dimmesdale's guilt affect his relationship to the people in his congregation?

20. How do the people respond when Dimmesdale tries to confess his sinfulness from the pulpit?

21. What has Dimmesdale's reputation become?

22. As his guilt weighs on him more and more, what practices does Dimmesdale take up?

23. What is the biblical remedy for his guilt? (Prov. 28:13; I John 1:9)

24. As he becomes weak and has hallucinations brought on by the abuse he is inflicting on his own body, what does he see?

25. Why are these particular visions significant?

ANSWERS TO QUESTIONS CHAPTERS 9-11

1. The barber took care of surgery, and an apothecary (druggist) took care of medicine.

2. The people feel that he is sacrificing his health by giving too much of himself to his work. They also feel that the world is not worthy of having him walking on it.

3. Some people believe that he has been plucked up from Europe by the hand of God and deposited on the soil of Boston.

4. Chillingworth's

5. The tapestry of David and Bathsheba represents the sin between Hester and Dimmesdale, and the tapestry of Nathan the prophet signifies the role Chillingworth plays.

6. The people feel he has changed from being calm, meditative and scholar-like into something ugly and evil. His appearance has taken on a darker duskiness that has led them to believe that he has some connection to Satan and the fires of hell.

7. He is digging into his heart "like a miner searching for gold."

8. He says he gathered them from a grave, growing from the heart of an unrepentant man.

9. the Judgment Day

10. He says that some cannot confess their sin in order to continue their service for God and bring glory to Him.

11. Dimmesdale's justification does not correspond at all with biblical teaching. The Bible teaches that to confess sin and forsake it is the only way to bring glory to God.

12. They hear the laughter of Pearl outside.

13. Because Pearl is the result of a sinful act herself, she refuses to submit herself to authority.

14. She recognizes that Chillingworth is satanic and that Dimmesdale is under his influence.

15. He will not submit himself to any earthly physician.

16. Chillingworth sneaks into the room, pulls open Dimmesdale's garment and sees something on his chest that causes him to become ecstatic.

17. He decides that he will become Dimmesdale's closest companion and most trusted friend, in order to be able to wreak his revenge with even more horror. In the beginning, he said he only wanted to reveal the father of the child; now he is plotting ways to increase his suffering.

18. He realizes that there is something threatening and evil, but then thinks that he is imagining this through his own guilt. He pushes his feelings to the back and tries to accept Chillingworth as a friend.

19. Because of his suffering and hypocrisy, he is more sensitive to the needs of the people in his congregation.

20. The people hold Dimmesdale up as being more holy, not believing what he is saying and thinking that if he sees something sinful in his pure soul, they must be even more sinful.

21. He has gained a reputation as the "Tongue of Flame."

22. He scourges himself with a whip, fasts for long periods of time, sits in the dark and contemplates his sin, then sits in the light looking in a mirror.

23. The biblical remedy is to confess sin and turn from it.

24. He sees demons, angels, old friends who are dead, his parents, and finally Hester leading Pearl by the hand and Pearl pointing at the scarlet letter.

25. These are significant because the demons and angels inhabit the spiritual world and accuse him; his parents and dead friends also are spiritual and accuse him from their graves. Hester, although she has never asked him to stand up and take his share of the punishment, has taken the entire brunt of the shame, and he knows that he has not taken responsibility for his sin with Hester or for his fatherhood of Pearl.

CHAPTER 12

Chapter 12 is a crucial chapter in the book. It is the central chapter, and all four of the main characters are seen together. Driven by guilt, Arthur Dimmesdale goes at midnight to the scaffold where Hester stood seven years earlier; she in her public display of guilt and he in the night where no one could see him except the one who knew of his bloody scourges (Chillingworth). Dimmesdale is suddenly overcome with the idea that the town will awaken in the morning to find him there, and will see a scarlet token on his naked breast. At this, he screams, believing that he will waken the entire town. However, no one hears him but Gov. Bellingham and his sister. Mistress Hibbins disappears, and the governor apparently thinks he is hearing things and puts out his light. As he stands on the scaffold, a light approaches, and it is Rev. Wilson, who is returning from the deathbed of Gov. Winthrop. Since Gov. Winthrop is a true historical figure who died in 1649, this sets the date for this episode. Dimmesdale speaks to Rev. Wilson (or imagines he does), but Wilson does not hear him and passes on by, much to Dimmesdale's relief. Dimmesdale is becoming so stiff he does not believe he will be able to descend the steps, and imagines he will be found there in the morning. He imagines the whole town coming out in the morning to find him standing on the scaffold, and the picture in his mind causes him to laugh.

His laughter is answered by a child's laughter; Hester and Pearl are also returning from Gov. Winthrop's deathbed, where Hester had been measuring him for burial clothing. He invites them to join him on the scaffold, and the three join hands, with Pearl forming the link between her parents. (Hawthorne calls her a conjunction). This is a climactic event. Pearl asks Dimmesdale if he will stand with her mother and her the next day at noon, and Dimmesdale answers that he will not stand with them the next day, but he will stand with them at the judgment day. Suddenly a meteor illuminates the sky, with the three of them on the scaffold; Arthur holding his hand over his heart, Hester with the scarlet letter and Pearl as the symbol that unites the two of them. Dimmesdale believes that the meteor makes a scarlet A in the sky, and Pearl withdraws her hand, pointing across the street at Roger Chillingworth. Dimmesdale asks Hester who he is, telling her that he terrifies him. Pearl says she knows who he is, but babbles nonsense into Dimmesdale's ear. Chillingworth then leads Dimmesdale down and takes him home. The next day his congregation believes that his sermon is the most powerful he has ever preached. The sexton brings him his glove, which was found on the scaffold, and they think that Satan had stolen it and placed it there. They also report that there was a strange letter A in the sky the night before, which has been interpreted to stand for "Angel," in regard to Gov. Winthrop's death.

VOCABULARY CHAPTER 12

somnambulism:	sleepwalking
culprits:	a person guilty of an offense or fault
obscure:	of little or no prominence or distinction
catarrh:	inflammation of a mucous membrane, esp. of the respiratory tract
defrauding:	to deprive of a right, money, or property by fraud
mockery:	ridicule; derision
penitence:	having regret for one's wrongdoing
trifled:	to deal with lightly or without due seriousness
expiation:	atone for; make amends or reparation for
bandying:	pass back and forth
multitudinous:	existing in great numbers; very numerous
clamor:	a loud uproar
excursions:	short trips or outings
conjectured:	to conclude or suppose from evidence insufficient to ensure reliability
grisly:	causing a shudder or feeling of horror
defunct:	no longer in existence
tumult:	a violent and noisy commotion
waxing:	to increase in extent
awry:	away from the expected or proper direction; amiss
askew:	crookedly
inextricable:	incapable of being disentangled, undone, or loosed
luminary:	a body, object, etc. that gives light; an important person
torrent:	a rushing, violent, or abundant stream of anything
half-torpid:	half inactive or sluggish
zenith:	highest point
egotism:	selfishness; self-centeredness
visionary:	belonging to or seen in a vision
grimly:	sternly; harshly
scurrilous:	grossly or obscenely abusive
portent:	an indication or omen of something about to happen

QUESTIONS CHAPTER 12

1. Where does Rev. Dimmesdale decide to go?

2. What time of day is it? Look up Ps. 32:3; Ps. 38:4; Ps. 44:15; Ps. 51:3; John 3:19. what does this say about Dimmesdale's condition?

3. Hawthorne says that, "No eye could see him, save that ever-wakeful one which had seen him in his closet, wielding the bloody scourge." Who is this?

4. What thought gives Rev. Dimmesdale "great horror of mind?

5. When he screams, what two people does he see in the governor's mansion?

6. When he sees a light approaching, who is it?

7. Where has this person been? Does he see Rev. Dimmesdale?

8. When Rev. Dimmesdale laughs at his mental image of people finding him there in the morning, what sound answers his laugh?

9. What does Pearl ask of Rev. Dimmesdale?

10. When does he say he will publicly stand with her and her mother?

11. What metaphor does Hawthorne use to refer to Pearl in this situation?

12. What does Rev. Dimmesdale think he sees in the sky?

13. At whom does Pearl point?

14. What is said about Rev. Dimmesdale's sermon the next day? Look at Rom. 1:16. From where does the power come that changes lives?

15. What does the sexton say about what was in the sky?

ANSWERS TO QUESTIONS CHAPTER 12

1. He goes to the scaffold where Hester stood when she was brought out of the prison when Pearl was a baby, seven years earlier.

2. It is midnight. Dimmesdale's sin has been weighing on him, and even the abuse he has been heaping on himself as punishment has not relieved his guilty conscience. John 3:19 says that when men's deeds are evil, they prefer darkness to light, so Dimmesdale has chosen to go to the scaffold in the darkness of night rather than in the light of day.

3. The thought that the entire universe could see a red mark on his naked chest causes him such horror that he screams. Apparently the red mark is a result of the scourging that he has been carrying out in his closet.

4. Roger Chillingworth

5. Gov. Bellingham & Mistress Hibbins

6. Rev. John Wilson

7. He has been sitting at the deathbed of Gov. Winthrop. He does not see Dimmesdale.

8. He hears the sound of a child laughing – it is little Pearl.

9. She asks if he will hold her hand and her mother's hand at noon the next day.

10. He says he will stand with them at the judgment day.

11. He calls her a conjunction.

12. A giant letter A

13. Roger Chillingworth

14. The people say it is the richest, most powerful he has ever preached, and many souls are brought to the truth through his sermon. The Word of God changes lives, not the power of the preacher.

15. The sexton says there was a letter A, which was interpreted to stand for angel because Gov. Winthrop had died that night – the sexton says he became an angel.

CHAPTERS 13-14

After seeing Dimmesdale's condition the night on the scaffold, Hester becomes concerned. She sees that he is nearing lunacy, and she knows that she holds the key to his sanity. Hawthorne explains how much Hester has changed in the ensuing years since we have last seen her. Because she had lived quietly, caring for the needs of others and asking nothing for herself, Hester's position in the community has changed somewhat. Although always an outcast, she is no longer the object of hatred and derision that she had been. Because she is the one called on when one is ill or in need of assistance, it is said that the letter A stands for "Able." She is considered to be a woman of strength, and the scarlet letter is considered to be imbued with magical powers – it is believed that it can protect her even from and Indian's arrow. In dealing with Pearl, Hester has felt so overwhelmed that she has considered killing Pearl and then committing suicide. Hester herself has ceased to have the appearance of a beautiful and desirable woman. Her hair is worn up under a hat, and she seems to have lost all of her femininity. She has become cold, lonely, and self-sufficient. Rather than bringing her to repentance, the scarlet letter has brought her to self-sufficiency. Hester decides she must face Chillingworth and demand to be released from her vow to keep his secret.

As soon as Hester finds the opportunity, she sends Pearl to play along the beach, and approaches Chillingworth, who is gathering herbs. He surprises her first by telling her that the magistrates have been talking about the possibility of allowing her to remove the scarlet letter. She informs him they do not have the authority to remove it. She stares at him, appalled by the changes that have taken place in his appearance. She finds there is an evil shining from his eyes, and feels he has transformed himself into a demon. When she tells him that she regrets making the promise to keep his secret, he asks what else she could have done, since he could have sent Dimmesdale to the gallows. She says it would have been better for him to have died than to be continually tortured by Chillingworth. Chillingworth asks her what evil he has done, since Dimmesdale would have wasted away within two years of his arriving if he had not kept him alive with medicine. Hester repeats that it would have been better for Dimmesdale to have died, and Chillingworth begins to enumerate all of the suffering he has been inflicting on the man. As he speaks of what he has been doing, and how he has been enjoying it, Chillingworth suddenly sees himself as the fiend he has become, and stops. Hester asks if he hasn't tortured the man enough, and he says no, he has increased the debt. He asks Hester what he was before, and what he is now, telling her he has become a fiend. When he asks who has made him a fiend, she says she has, and asks why he has not taken his revenge on her. He tells her he has left her to the scarlet letter. He asks what she wants, and she replies that she wants to reveal his secret. Hester tells him of her despair, that there is no hope for any of them. He tells her that he pities her, and she says she pities him. She urges him to forgive Dimmesdale and undo the evil that he has worked in his own soul, but he tells her it is not in him to do that. However, he releases her from her promise and tells her to do as she will about Dimmesdale. He then returns to gathering his herbs.

SUGGESTED ACTIVITIES CHAPTERS 13-14

1.   Have students make posters showing the transformation that has taken place in Roger Chillingworth over the seven years of the novel's course.

2.   Chillingworth is continually occupied with the gathering of herbs. Assign students to research herbs that would have been used during this time and available in the Boston area, then make a presentation in class.

3.   Ask students to choose one of the main characters and write a character study, telling the main strengths and weaknesses of this person.

VOCABULARY CHAPTERS 13-14

abased:	humiliated; degraded
groveled:	lie or crawl with the face downward and the body prostrate
fantastic:	extravagantly fanciful; lavish
apt:	suited to the purpose or occasion
prominence:	conspicuous
impeded:	obstructed; hindered
irksomeness:	annoying; irritating
conferred:	bestowed as a gift, favor or honor
gibe:	insulting remark
signification:	meaning; import; sense
meed:	reward
resolute:	determined; firmly set in purpose
despotic:	tyrannical; oppressive
benign:	of kindly disposition; gracious
propensity:	a natural tendency or inclination
constrain:	to force, compel or oblige
emancipated:	set free
speculation:	the contemplation or consideration of some subject
stigmatized:	set with some mark of disgrace or infamy
perilous:	dangerous
quietude:	tranquility; peacefulness
effluence:	something that flows out
obviated:	to anticipate and prevent
precipice:	a cliff with a vertical or overhanging face
chasm:	a deep gap or break
ghastly:	shockingly frightful or dreadful; horrible
semblance:	outward aspect or appearance
foreboded:	have a feeling of future evil
auspicious:	prosperous; fortunate
acquiescing:	submit or comply without protest
fragmentary:	broken; incomplete
agitated:	stirred up
discoursing:	talking; conversing
purport:	a purpose or intention
derisively:	ridiculing; mocking
extort:	to obtain by force, threat, , intimidation, or abuse of authority
behest:	a command; directive
peradventure:	chance, doubt, uncertainty
propinquity:	nearness in time or place
usurping:	to seize and hold by force or without legal right
avenged:	to take vengeance on
discern:	to see; recognize
bane:	a person or thing that ruins or spoils

QUESTIONS CHAPTERS 13-14

1. What does Hester find shocking about what she sees has been happening to Arthur Dimmesdale?

2. What does she know about what has been happening to him that no one else knows?

3. Because of her good works and capabilities, what have people come to believe the scarlet letter stands for?

4. What magical powers are attributed to the scarlet letter? To what other symbol do they compare it?

5. When Hawthorne says that everything is against Hester, he names two specific things. What are they?

6. Because of her loneliness and isolation from others, depression leads Hester to what kinds of thoughts?

7. Look up Eph. 2:12. What remedy could have eased Hester's hopelessness?

8. What does Hester feel about Arthur's mental condition?

9. What does it mean that "The scarlet letter had not done its office?"

10. In what is Hester trusting for her salvation?

11. Since they have last met in the prison seven years earlier, how have Hester's position and that of Roger Chillingworth changed?

12. What has Hester determined to do?

13. In the opening paragraph of chapter fourteen, what simile does Hawthorne use again to refer to Pearl? Why does he use this comparison so often?

14. With what news does Chillingworth surprise Hester when they first speak? What is her response?

15. As Hester observes Chillingworth, what does she tell him that he has transformed himself into?

16. Hawthorne uses the transformation of Chillingworth into a fiend as an extreme example of the consequences of evil. In this case, it is the result of revenge. Look at Rom. 12:19 and Heb. 10:30. What does the Bible say about taking revenge?

17. Why do you think this has taken such a terrible toll on Chillngworth?

18. As Chillingworth tells Hester of the pleasure he has taken from inflicting pain on the unsuspecting Dimmesdale, what suddenly happens to him?

19. What does Hester tell him he needs to do, both for Dimmesdale's sake, and also for his own?

20. Read Prov. 3:3; Eph. 4:32; Col. 3:13; I Th 5:15. What truth is there in what she has told him?

ANSWERS TO QUESTIONS CHAPTERS 13-14

1. She is shocked at the deteriorating of his mental condition.

2. Hester knows that his closest companion is also his most hated enemy.

3. "Able"

4. They believe that it can protect her from harm, even to the point of protecting her from an Indian's arrow. They compare it to a nun's cross.

5. The hostile world and the child's own nature

6. She considers killing Pearl and then committing suicide.

7. The only remedy for that kind of hopelessness is Christ.

8. She feels that he is on the verge of lunacy.

9. Although Hester conforms outwardly to the rules of society, she has never inwardly repented of her sin. The scarlet letter has not brought her to salvation.

10. She trusted in her own good works, her strength in the face of adversity and her pride.

11. Because of her good works, Hester has grown to a place of acceptance in the community, although she still lives in isolation and solitude. The people respect her and trust her, coming to her for help when they are in need. Chilllingworth, on the other hand, has become more and more repugnant, and has become more of an outcast. His obsession with revenge has isolated him and driven him away from the people even more than Hester's sin had.

12. She has decided that she must go to Chillingworth and demand to be released from her promise to keep his identity secret from Dimmesdale.

13. He compares her to a wild bird. Hawthorne continually uses this analogy because of the wild nature that exists in Pearl. She is a child with a lawless nature born from a sinful relationship.

14. He tells her that the magistrates have been discussing allowing her to remove the scarlet letter. She tells him it is not within their authority to remove it.

15. She tells him he has transformed himself into a fiend.

16. The Bible says that it is not our place to take revenge on one who has hurt us. We should leave that up to God. Vengeance belongs to God, not to man.

17. Chillingworth, like Satan, has taken upon himself the role that belongs only to God. When Hawthorne says that Roger Chillingworth was a striking evidence of man's faculty of transforming himself into a devil, if he will only, for a reasonable space of time, undertake a devil's office," this is what he was talking about.

18. As he is speaking, he suddenly sees himself as he is becoming, and is horrified.

19. She tells him he needs to forgive Dimmesdale.

20. The advice she has given him is biblical. Only through forgiving the one who has hurt him would he be able to find the ability to free himself from the hatred which had entangled him and transformed him.

CHAPTERS 15-16

As Hester walks away from Roger Chillingworth, she turns back and watches him bending down to gather his herbs, so stooped and bent that his beard almost touches the ground. Hester wonders if the evil in his being causes the very vegetation to become poisonous. She then begins to wonder how she could have ever married him, imagining that marrying him was a worse sin than committing adultery with Arthur Dimmesdale. She turns her attention to Pearl, who has been amusing herself along the seashore, finally using seaweed to make herself look like a mermaid, with eelgrass forming a green letter A on her chest. When Hester asks her if she knows why her mother wears the scarlet letter, Pearl answers that it is for the same reason that the minister holds his hand over his heart. At first, Hester thinks this is some disjointed childish reasoning, then realizes the truth in what Pearl has discerned. Hester has a moment of hesitation when she believes that Pearl may be old enough to take into her confidence, explain the circumstances of her birth and of her mother's suffering. However, Pearl persists in asking why she wears the scarlet letter, and why the minister holds his hand over his heart, and Hester tells Pearl that she wears the scarlet letter for the sake of the gold thread. It is the first time she has lied about the scarlet letter, and Hester feels guilty. Pearl refuses to let the matter drop, continuing the same line of questioning throughout the evening and even after she has been put to bed. Hester, exasperated, finally tells her that she will put her in a dark closet if she doesn't stop.

Hester determines that she needs to speak to Arthur Dimmesdale outside, in order to maintain an element of secrecy, so that his reputation will not be tarnished, and also in order to avoid Chillingworth being around. When she hears that he has been to visit the Apostle Eliot, one of his Indian converts, and will be returning the next day, she takes Pearl into the forest to await Dimmesdale's return.

As they cross into the forest, the scene is mainly dark and gloomy with a few glimmers of sunshine. Every time Hester nears the sunshine, it disappears. Hawthorne likens the forest to the "moral wilderness" in which Hester had been wandering for so long. Pearl tells her that the sunshine runs from her because of something that is on her bosom. She says it will not run from her, because she is a child, and does not have anything on her bosom yet. She runs to catch the sun, and Hester is caught up as it seems that Pearl does catch the sunshine. As Hester approaches, Pearl tells her it will go, but Hester puts out her hand, and the sunshine vanishes. Hester leads Pearl to sit down, and Pearl asks her to tell her a story about the Black Man. Pearl tells her she has heard that the scarlet letter is the Black Man's mark, and it glows like a red flame when her mother meets the Black Man in the forest at midnight. When she asks if that is true, Hester asks if she has ever awakened to find her mother gone. Pearl tells her no, but she would go with her to meet the Black Man. Hester tells her that she did meet the Black Man once, and the scarlet letter is his mark. As they are talking, Hester hears someone coming, and tells Pearl to go and play. Pearl asks if it is the Black Man, and wants to stay and see him. Hester tells her it is only the minister, and Pearl asks why he doesn't wear the Black Man's mark on the outside of his bosom, like she does. Hester tells her to go and play, but not too far, then watches Dimmesdale approach. He is leaning on a stick, very weak and seems to have no will to live.

VOCABULARY CHAPTERS 15-16

blighted: deteriorated or ruined
sere: withered
verdure: greenness
sedulous: diligent; persevering
deleterious: injurious to health
malignant: inclined to cause harm, suffering or distress
ominous: portending evil or harm
nuptial: of or pertaining to marriage
bask: to take great pleasure in;
reciprocated: to give, feel in return
impalpable: not able to be felt
foundered: to become wrecked; fail utterly
dexterity: skill using the hands
hornbook: a primer formerly used in teaching children to read
incongruity: inconsistent
capricious: erratic
waywardness: disobedience
petulant: showing sudden irritation
misdemeanors: instances of misbehaviors
precocity: unusually advanced or mature in mental development
acuteness: sharpness
scorn: open or unqualified contempt
acrid: sharply stinging or bitter
enigma: a puzzling occurrence or situation
innate: existing in one from birth
beneficence: doing good or causing good; beneficial
asperity: harshness or sharpness of tone
ulterior: intentionally kept concealed
imputed: charged with a fault
whither: to what place; where
betimes: before
primeval: of or pertaining to the first age or ages
imaged: pictured; imagined
extremity: the extreme limit
pensiveness: thoughtfulness or sadness
scintillating: to be animated; witty; sparkling
vivacity: animated; spirited
scrofula: a disease characterized by tumors in the glands of the neck,
                      under the chin, in the arm-pits, etc.
dell: a small, usually wooded valley
impending: about to happen
eddies: small whirlpools
loquacity: talkativeness
prattled: chatter or babble
cadence: the beat, rate, or measure of any rhythmic movement
lamentation: expression of grief

47

repining:	yearning for something
haggard:	gaunt, wasted or exhausted in appearance
despondency:	feeling or showing profound hopelessness
woefully:	wretched; unhappy
listlessness:	showing little interest in anything

QUESTIONS CHAPTERS 15-16

1. As Hester watches Chillingworth gathering herbs, what does she feel his evilness might cause the vegetation to become? What allusion does Hawthorne use in referring to Chillingworth?

2. What does Hester feel is moving along with Chillingworth?

3. When Hester remembers what it was like to be married to him, what does he say he needed from her?

4. How does she feel about her marriage to him in comparison to the sin she committed with Arthur Dimmesdale?

5. When Pearl talks with her mother about the meaning of the scarlet letter, she tells her it means the same thing as what gesture?

6. Hester momentarily believes that Pearl may be able to bring what into her life?

7. What lie does Hester tell Pearl?

8. What question does Pearl persist in asking, in order to upset her mother?

9. Where does Hester decide to go in order to speak to Rev. Dimmesdale about the true character of Roger Chillingworth?

10. Why does she choose this setting?

11. Where has Rev. Dimmesdale been?

12. How does Hawthorne use the setting as a metaphor for the psychological and spiritual battle that has been occurring in Hester's life?

13. How does Hawthorne use light and dark to contrast the difference in Hester and Pearl?

14. What does Pearl ask her mother to tell her a story about? Why?

15. Why does Hester tell Pearl that she cannot understand what the brook is saying?

16. When they hear someone approaching, and Hester tells Pearl it is the minister, what question does Pearl ask?

17. What is Arthur Dimmesdale's condition as he approaches?

18. An allegory is a story in which all of the elements are symbolic. Although *The Scarlet Letter* is not an allegory, it has allegorical elements. What is the Black Man symbolic of?

19. The symbolic reminder of Hester's past experiences that is present in the forest setting is what?

20. What does the mark of the Black Man symbolize?

ANSWERS TO QUESTIONS CHAPTERS 15-16

1. She thought his evilness might cause the vegetation to become poisonous. He alludes to him as a vampire ("would he spread bat's wings and flee away..")

2. She thinks there is an ominous shadow following him.

3. He needed the warmth of her smile to take off the chill of so many lonely hours among his books might be taking off of his heart.

4. She felt that marrying Chillingworth (actually Roger Prynne) was a worse sin than committing adultery with Arthur Dimmesdale.

5. Pearl tells her mother that the scarlet letter has the same meaning as the minister holding his hand over his heart.

6. Hester believes that Pearl might be able to bring comfort to soothe her sorrow.

7. She tells Pearl that she wears the scarlet letter for the sake of the gold thread.

8. She continually asks why the minister keeps his hand over his heart.

9. She decides that she will speak to him as he is walking in the forest.

10. She does not want to give any occasion for Dimmesdale to be accused of anything improper; she is afraid of Chillingworth trying to interfere; and she feels that only the outside gives enough room for them to breathe with what she has to tell him.

11. He has been to visit the Apostle Eliot, one of his Indian converts.

12. He says that it is like the moral wilderness through which she has been wandering for so long.

13. Pearl, who is lively and vivacious, is able to dance in the light and catch the light. Hester, who is always gloomy, causes the light to disappear whenever she comes near.

14. Pearl asks for a story about the Black Man because she has heard someone say that her mother's scarlet letter is the Black Man's mark, and it glows in the night when Hester goes to meet the Black Man at midnight in the forest.

15. Pearl has never known sorrow, so she cannot understand the sorrowful language of the brook.

16. Pearl asks why he does not wear the Black Man's mark on the outside of his bosom like her mother does.

17. He is so weak that he is leaning on a walking stick, he seems to be in a state of deep depression, not caring whether he lives or dies. Hester has not seen him in such a state of despair, because he has hidden the depths of his depression as he walked through the town, but here in the forest he is allowing his hopelessness to take control. He seems so exhausted that he can hardly put one foot in front of another, and would gladly lie down and allow the leaves to cover him up, forming a grave there in the forest.

18. The Black Man is symbolic of Satan.

19. The brook is the symbol of Hester's past experience.

20. the mark of the Black Man is sin.

CHAPTERS 17-19

As Hester calls out to Arthur Dimmesdale, he is not sure at first that there is someone really there. When he does see her, they find that they must touch each other before they reach an assurance that each is real. They sit silently on the mossy trunk of a fallen tree for a while, then address the question of whether or not each has found peace. Arthur says that, if he had been a man with no moral values he might have been able to live with the guilt, but he has not been able to. Hester brings up the reverence in which the people hold him, and the good works he does, but he tells her that these have not helped, because he knows the hypocrisy in which he is living, and the blackness of his soul. Hester is better off wearing the token of her sin on the outside for all to see. He tells her he wishes he had a friend in whom he could confide or even an enemy who would know him as he really is. She tells him that she will be such a friend to him, since she shares in his sin, and he has an enemy living in his very home. Hester then confesses that Roger Chillingworth is really her husband. Arthur becomes angry, saying that the revulsion he felt in his heart should have told him as much, and telling Hester that he will not forgive her. Hester pulls him to her breast and begs him to forgive her. She can endure the disapproval of the rest of society, but not the unforgiveness of this man she loves. He promises to forgive her, saying that the sin committed by Chillingworth is far worse than anything they have done. Hester brings up the concept that they had considered their relationship to have a consecration. They sit quietly for a while, until Arthur remarks that he cannot bear the thought of Chillingworth making his sin public. Hester does not believe that will happen, but Arthur also does not believe that he can continue to live with Chillingworth's torture any longer. Hester suggests he leave Boston, but he does not want to leave alone.

Hester, who has spent the past seven years outside of the major institutions of society, and has taken counsel only within her own heart and mind, becomes the strong one and declares that he will leave. Both Arthur and Hester feel exhilarated by the decision, and he declares that he has been virtually born again – he came into the forest "sick, sin-stained, sorrow-blackened," and met Hester , "my better angel." Now he feels he has found joy again. Hester impulsively takes off the scarlet letter and throws it away, almost into the brook, as a gesture of their newly found lives. As they sit making their plans, Hester tells him she wants him to get to know Pearl – that he will love her like Hester does. Arthur is afraid of Pearl, as he is of most children. Hester calls Pearl to her, and Pearl comes, but hesitates when she sees the minister sitting with her mother.

Arthur tells Hester that, as he has seen Pearl with Hester in the town, he has feared that he has seen his "own features repeated on her face," and thought someone might notice she is his child. Hester warns him not to seem too eager with Pearl, or he will upset her. He tells her that children don't, as a rule like him, but Pearl has been kind to him twice – once at the governor's mansion when she was three, and once when they stood on the scaffold. As Pearl approaches, she will not cross the brook, no matter how persistent Hester is in trying to convince her. Finally, Pearl begins to point at her mother's breast and throws a tantrum. Hester realizes that the child is distraught because she is not wearing the scarlet letter. She tells Pearl to pick up the letter and bring it to her, but Pearl demands that Hester come and get it. Pearl comes and kisses Hester, then kisses the scarlet letter. She tells her to greet the minister, and Pearl asks if he will walk hand in hand with them in the town. When

Hester tells her no, but in the future he will, Pearl asks again why he always keeps his hand over his heart. Trying to make things better, Arthur kisses Pearl on the forehead, and she promptly runs to the brook and washes the kiss from her face, ending their time together.

SUGGESTED ACTIVITIES CHAPTERS 17-19

1. Make pictures representing the visual aspects of this scene: the gloomy forest, the babbling brook, the sunlight that dances only on Pearl.

2. Have students write a skit and present this scene in class.

3. Have students create a diorama of this scene.

VOCABULARY CHAPTERS 17-19

disembodied:	a soul without a body
estranged:	kept at a distance; alienated
devoid:	without
wretch:	a person of despicable or base character
interpose:	to place between
malevolent:	wishing evil or harm on others
contiguity:	touching; in contact
misanthropy:	hatred of mankind
grievous:	causing grief or great sorrow
striven:	struggled vigorously
transfiguration:	a change in outward form or appearance
indelicacy:	offensive to decency
abyss:	a bottomless pit
dolefully:	sorrowfully
satiating:	satisfying to the full
cumber:	to hinder; hamper; burden
freight:	to load
habituated:	to accustom to a particular situation
latitude:	freedom from narrow restrictions
colloquy:	a conversational exchange; conference
transgressed:	violated a law; sinned
minuteness:	attentive to the smallest details
trammeled:	restrained
fretting:	wearing away by irritation
extenuation:	to make or try to make seem less serious by offering excuses
exquisite:	intense; acute
expiating:	atoning for; making amends for
citadel:	a fortress
irrevocably:	not to be revoked or recalled
solace:	comfort
exhilarating:	invigorating
temperament:	the combination of mental and emotional traits of a person
stigma:	a stain or reproach on one's reputation
transmuting:	changing from one nature or condition to another
subjugated:	brought under control; mastered
denizens:	inhabitants; residents
choleric:	easily angered
adorn:	to decorate
nymph:	a class of lesser mythological deities inhabiting the seas, rivers, trees, or mountains
dryad:	a nymph of the woods
hieroglyphic:	a system of writing consisting of pictographs
picturesqueness:	visually charming or quaint
tantalizing:	provoking expectation, interest, or desire

inured:	toughened or hardened by use or exposure
mollified:	softened in feeling or temper; pacify; appease
entreaties:	earnest requests; pleas
gesticulating:	to make or use gestures in an animated or excited manner
contortions:	drawing out of shape
cankered:	corrupted
inevitable:	unable to be avoided

QUESTIONS CHAPTERS 17-19

1. What is Rev. Dimmesdale's first impression when Hester calls out to him?

2. How do the two people assure each other that they are talking to someone alive?

3. Once they have talked of minor things, what is the important question that is asked?

4. What does Arthur say he wishes the people's reverence would turn into?

5. Why does he believe that Hester must be happier than he?

6. How does Dimmesdale's thinking compare to Prov. 28:13? What further step does he need to take?

7. What is Dimmesdale's response when Hester reveals the true identity of Chillingworth?

8. When he changes his mind, what does he say to her about Chillingworth's actions?

9. What justification did Hester and Arthur give themselves for their relationship seven years earlier?

10. Read Rom. 7:3; II. I Cor. 6:18; Col. 3:5; I Th. 4:3; Pet. 2:14-15. What do these verses say about the position taken by Hester and Arthur?

11. What does Arthur tell Hester she must be for him?

12. What suggestion does Hester give to Arthur in order to free him from the bondage he is under?

13. What does Hester do that is symbolic of their new life together?

14. Why does Arthur stay away from children?

15. How does he feel toward Pearl? On what two occasions has Pearl showed special tenderness toward him?

16. What has he feared people might see in Pearl?

17. What metaphor does Hawthorne use in this chapter to represent Pearl as the uniting force between Hester and Arthur?

18.   Why does Pearl throw a temper tantrum?

19.   What does Pearl ask of the minister?

20.   What is Pearl's response to her father's kiss on her forehead?

ANSWERS TO QUESTIONS CHAPTERS 17-19

1. He thinks that he is seeing a ghost.

2. They touch each other.

3. "Have you found peace?"

4. He says he wishes their reverence would turn into scorn and hatred.

5. He thinks Hester must be happier because her sin is out in the open, not hidden. He is constantly dealing with the fact that he is a hypocrite.

6. He can't prosper as long has he hides his sin. If he wants to be free from the guilt, he needs to confess his sin.

7. He becomes angry and tells her he cannot forgive her.

8. He tells her that Chillingworth's sin is worse than theirs. Of course, this is a justification. Sin is sin.

9. They told themselves their relationship was consecrated.

10. Hester was married to another man at the time, so they were guilty of adultery, and both were aware of this. Arthur, although he was an educated Bible scholar who knew what the Scripture had to say about adultery, and carried a greater responsibility as her pastor, had chosen to justify his sin anyway, and try to make it something it was not.

11. He tells her she must be strong for him.

12. She suggests he go somewhere away from Boston.

13. She takes off the scarlet letter and throws it away from them, then lets her hair down, allowing her femininity to reappear.

14. He stays away from children because they seem to distrust him.

15. He is afraid of Pearl. However, she has shown him kindness at Gov. Bellingham's mansion and when they stood on the scaffold.

16. He has been afraid people might see some resemblance to him.

17. Hawthorne calls Pearl a "visible tie" that united Hester and Dimmesdale.

18. Pearl throws a tantrum because her mother is not wearing the scarlet letter.

19. She asks if he will walk hand in hand with her mother and her into the town. Pearl's questions both about and to her father continually emphasize his hypocrisy.

20. She goes to the brook and washes the kiss off her forehead.

CHAPTERS 20-24

As Rev. Dimmesdale leaves Hester and Pearl and returns to the town, he has a renewed energy grown from his plans to leave with Hester. He is excited at the prospect that he will still be able to preach the Election Day sermon, which is three days later, telling himself that no one will say that he has left his duties unperformed. Of course, in reality, Dimmesdale is the same prideful, hypocritical sinner he has been all along. As he re-enters the town, he feels as if everything has changed, even though he has only been gone for two days. His plans with Hester have allowed his heart to sink deeper into the depths of sinfulness, as seen in his reactions to his congregants as he walks. First he meets the oldest deacon and is tempted to make some blasphemous suggestion to him; next he meets the eldest female member of the congregation, and desires to whisper some argument against the immortality of the human soul into her ear; third is the youngest female member to whom he considers making some lewd suggestion, but is instead rude. He is finally tempted to teach some Puritan children curse words. He meets Mistress Hibbins, who makes a remark about his visit to the forest, with an offer to accompany him to visit the Black Man. He wonders to himself if he has sold his soul to Satan. When he returns to his apartment, he is met by Chillingworth, who tells him he appears pale and offers medicine. Dimmesdale tells him he feels he will no longer be needing his medicine. He sends for a servant to bring food and begins to eat ravenously. He puts his previously finished sermon into the fire, and begins a new sermon.

As the day of the installation of the new governor dawns, Hawthorne sets the festive atmosphere of the celebration in contrast to Hester's solemn placidity. As Hester arrives in the town, she is her usual impassive self outwardly, but she experiences an undercurrent of excitement inwardly as she anticipates being able to escape the power of the scarlet letter.

Pearl, always the hyperactive child, senses the difference in her mother's mood and is more agitated than usual. She also does not understand why all work has come to a standstill and everyone is playing. She asks if the minister will be there, and if he will hold out both his hands to her like he did at the brook side. Hester tells her he will be there, but he won't greet her and Pearl shouldn't greet him. Pearl, ever the insightful child, remarks that he is a strange, sad man who will hold their hands in the night and in the forest, but not in the light of day. She again remarks how strange it is that he keeps his hand over his heart all the time. Hawthorne then describes the different people represented in the scene, including the sailors from the ship. The commander of the ship is seen in the company of Roger Chillingworth. The sailor proceeds to Hester and tells her that Chillingworth has booked passage on the same vessel that she and Dimmesdale have already purchased passage on to England.

Before Hester can consider what to do, the procession enters the marketplace. Arthur is marching with such vigor and energy that the entire community is amazed. Hester hopes to be able to catch Arthur's eye, to warn him of the problem she has discovered. However, he is so caught up in his thoughts of his sermon that he seems to be in another world, and she is angry with him. Pearl asks if that is the same minister who kissed her by the brook, and Hester warns her not to talk in the marketplace of what happens in the forest. Pearl asks what would happen if she ran up and asked the minister to kiss her now. Would he clasp his hand over his heart and scowl at her? Hester cautions that kisses are not for the marketplace. Mistress Hibbins approaches Hester and intimates that she knows what occurred between Hester and Arthur on the forest path. Hester admonishes her for saying such a thing, but Mistress Hibbins says that what is on the minister's heart will come to the light. Pearl asks her if she knows what it is. By this time, the sermon has begun, and the crowd is held spellbound. Hester is stuck by the scaffold, with a void between her and everyone else. Pearl, meanwhile, is still dancing and flitting among the participants in the festivities. The commander of the ship tells her to take a message to her mother that Chillingworth will bring Dimmesdale on board the ship, so Hester only needs to take care of herself and Pearl. As the people outside the church become bored with other activities, they begin to gather around Hester, pointing and jeering as they have not done in years.

As Rev. Dimmesdale's sermon ends and the people leave, they are enraptured with his message, believing his words are as inspired as those of the Old Testament prophets. The procession makes its way away from the church, moving toward the town hall where there is to be a meal. Rev. Dimmesdale is so weak that he is literally staggering, moving like an infant taking its first steps. Rev. Wilson moves to help him, but he waves him away and calls for Hester and Pearl. Pearl wraps her arms around his legs, and he asks for Hester to help him up onto the scaffold. When Chillingworth realizes what Dimmesdale intends, he is horrified, and tries to stop him. The four main characters mount the steps to the scaffold together, and Chillingworth tells

him there is nowhere else in the whole world he can escape him but on this scaffold. Dimmesdale then announces to the entire community that he should have stood on the scaffold with Hester seven years earlier, and he bears the same guilty mark as she, but his had been hidden. He pulls aside his garments to reveal something on his chest. Chillingworth declares, "Thou hast escaped me!" Pearl finally kisses Dimmesdale, acknowledging her father, and Dimmesdale dies in Hester's arms.

There is disagreement as to whether the mark on Dimmesdale's heart has been caused by his own abuse, by Chillingworth, or by his guilt working from the inside out. Some deny seeing anything at all. Losing the object of his revenge, Chillingworth withers up and dies within a year, leaving a large amount of property to Pearl. Hester and Pearl disappear, but Hester returns some years later after Pearl is grown, and moves back into her cottage. She willingly returns to wearing the scarlet letter. No on knows what has happened to Pearl, but Hester receives rich gifts from Europe, and is seen embroidering rich clothing for a baby. Hester becomes a counselor for women who experience all kinds of sorrow or are going through trials or are outcasts. When Hester dies she is buried next to Dimmesdale so that they shared a tombstone, but their graves do not touch.

VOCABULARY CHAPTERS 20-24

vicissitude:	regular change or succession of one state or thing to another
antiquity:	ancient times
intrusive:	tending to come in without permission
duplicity:	deceitfulness
vexed:	irritated; annoyed
rendered:	made; caused to be
exemplary:	commendable
apprehend:	understand
irrefragable:	not to be disputed or contested
uncouth:	rude, uncivil, boorish
plashy:	puddles
gable:	triangular shape enclosed by or masking the end of a roof that slopes downward from a central ridge
obtrusive:	having a disposition to impose oneself or one's opinions on others
mutability:	subject to change
phenomenon:	something that is remarkable or extraordinary
dynasty:	a sequence of rulers from the same family or group
incited:	stimulated to action
blasphemous:	to speak irreverently of God
sanctified:	to make holy
pithy:	brief, forceful and meaningful in expression
transitory:	lasting only a short time
archfiend:	a chief fiend; Satan
ransacked:	search thoroughly and vigorously
dissolute:	indifferent to moral restraints; immoral
decorum:	proper conduct
potentate:	a person possessing great power, such as a ruler or monarch
gratuitous:	being without cause or justification
recompense:	to pay or give compensation for
ravenous:	extremely hungry
wormwood:	something bitter, grievous, or extremely unpleasant
aloes:	medicine used as a laxative
perpetually:	continuing or enduring forever
languor:	lack of energy
cordial:	a stimulating medicine
manifestation:	state of being seen by the eye
effervescence:	showing enthusiasm, excitement, or liveliness
unwonted:	unusual
appliances:	any instrument or device for a particular purpose or use
minstrel:	a medieval poet, singer, and musician
gleeman:	a musician
Merry Andrew:	a buffoon; a clown
jocularity:	characterized by joking
repressed:	to keep down or suppress
posterity:	future generations

desperadoes: bold, reckless outlaws
ferocity: savagely fierce or cruel
scruple: moral or ethical consideration that constrains one's behavior
aquavitae: strong alcoholic liquor
depredations: acts of robbery and violence
tempestuous: stormy; turbulent
buccaneer: a pirate
probity: integrity and uprightness; honesty
piety: reverence for God
disreputable: having a bad reputation; dishonorable
animadversion: an unfavorable or critical comment
profusion: great quantity
surmounted: to be on top or above
galliard: brisk; active
scurvy: a disease caused by a lack of vitamin C
consternation: sudden, alarming amazement or dread that results in confusion
contiguous: touching; in contact
clarion: brilliantly clear
mercenary: working or acting merely for money
martial: inclined or disposed to war
Knights Templars: military order during the Crusades
integrity: uncompromised honesty; soundness of moral character
endowments: the property, funds, etc, with which a person or institution is furnished
compeers: associates; equals
sobriety: seriousness
fortitude: mental and emotional strength
divine: a priest or cleric
inducements: incentives
aspiring: longing, aiming, or seeking ambitiously
abstracted: thought of apart from concrete reality
scowled: affected an angry expression
stomacher: an ornament or support to the breast, worn by females
necromancer: one who practices divination through invocation of the dead
trifle: something of little value, importance or consequence
auditor: one who listens
proximity: nearness
pathos: pity
plaintiveness: expressing sorrow or melancholy
orb: a sphere or globe
undulating: moving in a wave-like motion
indefatigable: incapable of being tired out
audacity: shameless boldness
perplexity: bewilderment
boorish: rude; unmannerly
unscrupulous: not restrained by morals; unprincipled
centrifugal: directed outward from the center

languidly: lacking vigor or vitality
oracles: those who deliver authoritative and influential
                  pronouncements
symphonious: a harmonious combination of elements
apotheosized: deified; glorified
intimations: indicated or made known indirectly
appalled: filled with horror or fear
meridian: noonday
fathomless: too deep to understand
remorse: sorrow for wrongdoing
repose: rest; tranquility
nugatory: trifling or worthless
consummation: the state of being complete
bequeathed: disposed of property in a will
impediments: obstacles
armorial: pertaining to a coat of arms
escutcheon: a shield or shield-like surface on which a coat of arms is
                  depicted

QUESTIONS CHAPTERS 20-24

1. What is the final destination on which Hester and Arthur settle? Why?

2. Why is Arthur pleased about the amount of time that will elapse before they can leave?

3. Look at James 1:8. How does Hawthorne's description of Dimmesdale echo the truth of this verse?

4. What physical changes have come over Dimmesdale as he leaves the forest and returns to the town?

5. What temptations does Dimmesdale meet as he enters the town?

6. Read the first chapter of Romans. How does the progression of sinfulness in man detailed in this chapter parallel Dimmesdale's experience?

7. Who speaks to Arthur, letting him know she is aware of his meeting with Hester in the forest?

8. When Dimmesdale returns to his apartment, what does Chillingworth sense about him?

9. As they come to the celebration on Election Day, what comment does Pearl make about Dimmesdale?

10. How is Hester different as she appears in the market place for the Election Day festivities?

11. How does Hester's emotional state affect Pearl?

12. Besides the Puritans of Boston, what two other groups of people are present at the celebration?

13. What does the shipmaster tell Hester?

14. What is Arthur Dimmesdale like as he marches in the procession?

15. What causes Hester to become angry?

16. As Dimmesdale is preaching, where is Hester? What is happening to her?

17. As they leave the church, what do the people say about his sermon?

18. What is Dimmesdale's condition?

19. Where does he go? Who tries to stop him?

20. What does Chillingworth tell him? Why is this true?

21. What does Dimmesdale tell the people?

22. What are the three explanations for the mark on his chest?

23. What happens to Chillingworth? Why?

24. What happens to Pearl?

25. Why does Hester come back?

ANSWERS TO QUESTIONS CHAPTERS 20-24

1.   Europe; Due to his health and scholarly tendencies, it would be easier for him to disappear there.

2.   It will allow him to preach the Election Day sermon three days later

3.   A "double-minded man is unstable in all his ways." Hawthorne depicts a man who has deceived himself with his own hypocrisy to the point that he is mentally unstable, and he does not even realize the idiocy of what he is considering.

4.   He is excited, invigorated, full of energy, even though he had been to the point of dropping dead with exhaustion in the forest.

5.   First he meets the oldest deacon and is tempted to make some blasphemous suggestion to him; then he meets the eldest female member of the congregation, and desires to whisper some argument against the immortality of the human soul into her ear; next is the youngest female member to whom he considers making some lewd suggestion, but is instead rude. He is finally tempted to teach some Puritan children curse words.

6.   Once he opens himself up to sin, he becomes more willing to sin, and the suggestion of sin takes hold in him. Sexual sins are especially dangerous, blinding the mind and hardening the heart to the Word of God.

7.   Mistress Hibbins

8.   He realizes that Dimmesdale no longer regards him as a trusted friend.

9.   She says that he is a strange, sad man, who will hold their hands in the forest and on the scaffold in the dark, but not in the daylight among the people.

10. Although she appears the same on the outside, there is a current of excitement within her as she contemplates her plans to run away with Arthur and get rid of the scarlet letter forever.

11. Pearl is even more agitated than usual.

12. Indians and sailors

13. He tells Hester that Chillingworth has also booked passage on the ship with them.

14. Dimmesdale is more energetic and lively than he has been in years. He has no feebleness in his step, and his hand is not over his heart. He also seems to be entirely carried away by his thoughts of his own sermon; he is oblivious to the people gathered in the marketplace.

15. Hester had hoped that she could make some eye contact with Arthur, in order to give him some indication of the peril they are now in. However, his thoughts are not on her at all, and this causes her to be jealous and angry.

16. Hester is standing by the scaffold. A group of strangers have gathered around her and are using her as an object of derision and insult. Because the people of Boston have left her alone for several years, this is the first time in years this has happened.

17. The people believe that no one has ever spoken in as high, wise and holy as spirit as Dimmesdale spoke that day. They also feel that there was an undertone to his message which seems to indicate he will soon die and go to heaven.

18. He can barely walk; he is staggering and tottering like a weakened infant.

19. He goes to Hester and Pearl at the scaffold. Chillingworth tries to stop him.

20. Chillingworth tells him there is no other place in the earth where he could have escaped him. This is true because Chillingworth only has had a hold over him as long as his sin was secret. Once he confesses his sin to the world, Chillingworth has nothing with which to torture him.

21. Dimmesdale tells the people that he should have stood with Hester 7 years earlier; that while she has walked openly with the mark of her sin there has been one among them who has had the mark of sin but has kept it hidden.

22. Chillingworth dies within a year. He has been so consumed with revenge that once the source of his revenge is removed he has no reason to live and his existence ends. He leaves all of his property both in New England & Europe to Pearl, making her a very wealthy child.

23. The three possible explanations are:

a. the bloody scourges Dimmesdale has been inflicting on himself
b. Chillingworth's medicine   (some poison)
c. guilt gnawing from the inside of his heart out

24.   Hester takes Pearl to Europe, and no one knows for sure what happens to her, but from the gifts that arrive for Hester and the baby clothing Hester embroiders, it would appear that Pearl has married and is living happily in Europe.

25.   Hester comes back because she still feels connected to this place through her sin. She still feels a need to do penance. Always the self-sufficient woman, she continues to trust in her good works to make amends for what she has done wrong and buy her salvation. Coming back also allows her to be buried next to Arthur, the only man she has loved.

VOCABULARY TEST CHAPTERS 1-3
THE SCARLET LETTER

I. **Multiple Choice: Circle the letter of the correct answer:**

1. At the beginning of the story, there was a great **throng** gathered around the scaffold:
   a. tomb
   b. an ideal place
   c. moral excellence
   d. crowd

2. Which of the following does **not** refer to the **face:**
   a. physiognomies
   b. demeanor
   c. visages
   d. furrowed

3. Which of the following does **not** belong:
   a. brazen
   b. haughty
   c. melancholy
   d. hussy

4. The stranger had come from a **sojourn** among the Indians:
   a. temporary stay
   b. high station
   c. building
   d. messenger

5. Hester was forced to stand on the scaffold in her hour of **ignominy**:
   a. moral excellence
   b. personal disgrace; dishonor
   c. regret for wrongdoing
   d. decorations

6. Hester's **demeanor** gave no indication of sorrow for her sin:
   a. weakness
   b. doctrinal statement
   c. facial appearance; conduct
   d. stubbornness

7. The stranger's **heterogeneous** costume drew attention to him:
   a. not practical
   b. brightly colored
   c. exceptional or abnormal
   d. composed of parts of different kinds

8. Hester continued in her **obstinacy** when it came to not revealing the father's name:
   a. stubbornness
   b. accustomed to
   c. without a particular feeling or sensation
   d. proud; arrogant

9. Hester was led from the prison by the **beadle**:
   a. sheriff
   b. clerk
   c. messenger or crier of the court
   d. secretary

10. The Rev. Wilson was a **venerable** person:
    a. proud
    b. respectable
    c. weak
    d. sad

11. Gov. Bellingham was a **magistrate**:
    a. one who has broken the law
    b. without visible means of support
    c. one charged with administering the law
    d. one who is skilled in giving speeches

12. Hester's sentence had been handed down by the legal **tribunal**:
    a. messenger
    b. civil officer
    c. multitude of people
    d. court of justice

13. Which of the following does **not** belong:
    a. venerable
    b. ignominy
    c. eminence
    d. virtue

14. Rev. Dimmesdale was a man who was apt to be **tremulous**:
    a. exceptional or abnormal
    b. disdainfully proud
    c. characterized by trembling
    d. heavy; massive

15. While Hester was on the scaffold she maintained an attitude of **indifference**:
    a. lack of interest or concern
    b. a gloomy state of mind
    c. weakness
    d. stubbornness

16. In the imagination of the people, the scarlet letter seemed to get its scarlet color from the **infernal** pit:
    a. temporary
    b. unfavorable
    c. hellish
    d. ideal

17. Hester had embellished the scarlet A with **flourishes** of gold thread:
    a. authority
    b. decorations
    c. lack of concern
    d. purpose or intention

18. Rev. Wilson used the occasion for a **discourse** on sin:
    a. a multitude of people
    b. something that is improper
    c. raised platform
    d. sermon

19. The stranger made a movement that was **imperceptible**:
    a. very slight or subtle
    b. one within another
    c. without regret for wrongdoing
    d. becoming quiet

20. The man had an **impending** brow:
    a. wrinkled
    b. threatening
    c. spiteful
    d. lacking concern

II.   Matching: Place the letter of the correct answer in the blank:

1.____Utopia   A. signified by some visible object

2.____invariably   B. the quality of being improper

3.____sepulchers   C. to divine or predict

4.____beetle-browed   D. hoop petticoat

5.____ponderous   E. an ideal place or state

6.____augured   F. tomb, grave, or burial place

7.____betokened   G. and idle person without visible means of support

8.____vagrant   H. of great weight; heavy, massive

9.____impropriety   I. having prominent brows

10.___farthingale   J. without changing

III. Matching: Place the letter of the correct answer in the blank:

1.____rotundity   A. to believe, trust, think or suppose

2.____purport   B. conduct; behavior

3.____malefactress   C. intended to regulate personal habits on moral or
                         religious grounds

4.____hussy   D. a purpose or intention

5.____trow   E. female person who violates the law

6.____abashed   F. disappearing gradually; fading away

7.____sumptuary   G. wooden framework with holes for hands, feet and head

8.____evanescent   H. full toned or sonorous

9.____deportment   I. a brazen or disreputable woman

10.___pillory   J. made embarrassed or ashamed

IV. True/False: Write T or F in the Blank:

1._____ A Papist is one who belongs to the Baptist Church.

2._____ Someone with a furrowed visage and weak optics would be probably be young.

3. _____ Phantasmagoric, or scary, images passed before Hester as she stood on the scaffold.

4. _____ Roger Chillingworth was a man of sagacity.

5. _____ Aspect, mien, demeanor and deportment are words that are related.

6. _____ The cries of the baby subsided once Hester left the bright sunshine and went back
    into the prison.

7._____ Hester's parents had not been enough created enough of a remonstrance to keep
    her from sinning.

8. _____ Rev. Dimmesdale admired Hester because of her obstinacy in refusing to reveal the
    name of the baby's father.

9. _____ When Hawthorne says the balcony was appended to the building, he means it was

added.

10._____ When Hawthorne says Hester's mind was preternaturally active, it means she has

the mind of a preschooler.

VOCABULARY TEST CHAPTERS 1-3 ANSWERS
THE SCARLET LETTER

I. Multiple Choice:

1. d
2. b
3. c
4. a
5. b
6. c
7. d
8. a
9. c
10. b
11. c
12. d
13. b
14. c
15. a
16. c
17. b
18. d
19. a
20. b

II. Matching:

1. E
2. J
3. F
4. I
5. H
6. C
7. A
8. G
9. B
10. D

III.   Matching:

1. H
2. D
3. E
4. I
5. A
6. J
7. C
8. F
9. B
10. G

IV.   True/False:

1. F
2. F
3. F
4. T
5. T
6. F
7. T
8. T
9. T
10. F

VOCABULARY TEST CHAPTERS 4-6
THE SCARLET LETTER

I.   Multiple Choice: Circle the letter of the correct answer:

1. Which of the two combinations of words are antonyms?
    a. singular and peremptory
    b. enjoin and retribution
    c. perpetrate and quell
    d. morbid and lurid

2. Reasoning with someone by way of warning or rebuke is:
    a. efficacy
    b. gesticulation
    c. retribution
    d. expostulation

3. Which words are synonyms?
    a. vulgar and plebeian
    b. incredulity and inscrutable
    c. pomp and ruff
    d. scourging and anathemas

4. Punishment undergone as penitence for sin is called:
    a. superfluous
    b. penance
    c. commiseration
    d. prolific

5. Pearl was willfully disobedient; in other words, she acted:
    a. disporting
    b. vulgarly
    c. placidly
    d. contumaciously

6. Hester **procured** the most luxurious cloth for the clothing she made for Pearl:
    a. received into the mind
    b. obtained
    c. asserted or affirmed with confidence
    d. saturated deeply

7. Chillingworth told Hester to reveal her **paramour**:
    a. Indian chief
    b. person who originates something
    c. illicit lover
    d. good luck charm

8. The children of the town **reviled** Pearl in the way they spoke to her:
   a. spoke abusively
   b. whipped
   c. questioned
   d. helped

9. Hester's clothing was very **ascetic**:
   a. stately or splendid
   b. dark; shadowy
   c. soiled; tarnished
   d. austere; simple

10. Chillingworth told the jailer that he would be able to make Hester more **amenable** the authorities:
    a. make sore by rubbing
    b. effectiveness
    c. willing to yield; agreeable
    d. to be aware of

11. Pearl's outward appearance underwent a constant **mutability**:
    a. punishment
    b. change or alteration
    c. expression of sympathy
    d. gloomy; dark

12. Hester was in a **labyrinth** of doubt:
    a. peace of mind
    b. prison
    c. trap
    d. maze

13. Pearl was a child subject to **caprice**:
    a. being able to believe
    b. speaking abusively
    c. sudden unpredictable change
    d. helping others

14. Pearl sees the Puritan children playing like they are **scourging** Quakers:
    a. beating with a whip
    b. showing kindness toward
    c. cursing
    d. reasoning with

15. The action of feeling or expressing sympathy for is:
    a. pomp
    b. insidious
    c. penance
    d. commiseration

16. Hester tried to **succor** those who were in greater need than she:
    a. treat with disdain
    b. help or relieve in difficulty
    c. intend to entrap
    d. cheat

17. Hawthorne says that Pearl's life came from the "**inscrutable** decree of Providence:"
    a. sudden
    b. leaving no opportunity for denial
    c. capacity for producing a desired result
    d. not easily understood; mysterious

18. Which of the following does **not** refer to something dark, gloomy, black:
    a. sable
    b. sprite
    c. somber
    d. morbid

19. The only time Pearl exhibited **placidity** was during her sleep:
    a. peacefulness
    b. gloominess
    c. willfully disobedient
    d. willing to yield

20. Chillingworth calls Pearl a **misbegotten** child:
    a. disobedient
    b. abusive
    c. disabled
    d. illegitimate

II. Matching: Place the letter of the correct answer in the blank:

1.____sagamores   A. medieval form of chemistry attempting to find the elixir of life

2.____intimated   B. obsolete term for a physician

3.____alchemy   C. period of time marked by distinctive features

4.____draught   D. hint; imply; suggest

5.____efficacy   E. an action in return for a service, kindness, etc.

6.____leech   F. drink in hearty enjoyment

7.____requital   G. Indian chief

8.____quaff   H. capacity to produce the desired result

9.____feigned   I. the quantity of liquor drank at once

10.___epoch   J. pretended

III. Matching: Place the letter of the correct answer in the blank:

1.____wrought   A. characterized by indulgence in luxury

2.____enjoin   B. take in and incorporate as one's own; absorb

3.____wottest   C. prohibit or restrain

4.____lurid   D. stately or splendid display

5.____sufficed   E. worked

6.____assimilate   F. gruesome; horrible; revolting

7.____fain   G. person or thing that originates something

8.____progenitors   H. to know; be aware of

9.____pomp   I. gladly; willingly

10.___voluptuous   J. to be enough or adequate

ANSWERS TO VOCABULARY TEST CHAPTERS 4-6
THE SCARLET LETTER

I.   Multiple Choice:

1. c
2. d
3. a
4. b
5. d
6. b
7. c
8. a
9. d
10. c
11. b
12. d
13. c
14. a
15. d
16. b
17. d
18. b
19. a
20. d

II.   Matching:

1. G
2. D
3. A
4. I
5. H
6. B
7. E
8. F
9. J
10. C

III.   Matching:

1. E
2. C
3. H
4. F
5. J
6. B
7. I
8. G
9. D
10. A

VOCABULARY CHAPTERS 7-8
THE SCARLET LETTER

I.   **Multiple Choice: Circle the letter of the correct answer:**

1. Pearl had an attitude that was **imperious**:
   a. showing ill health
   b. desiring to do good
   c domineering; dictatorial
   d. morally upright

2. Hester was **impelled** to go to the Governor's Mansion for two reasons:
   a. drive or urge forward
   b. criticize
   c. banish; exile
   d. to leap or skip

3. This was a time of **pristine** simplicity:
   a. not planned beforehand
   b. bold
   c. occupying a special position
   d. having its original purity

4. Which of the following does **not** refer to a part of a knight's armor:
   a. cuirass
   b. greaves
   c. gorget
   d. tome

5. Pearl was a **dauntless** child:
   a. weak
   b. ghostly in appearance
   c. bold; not intimidated
   d. abnormally thin

6. Which set of words are synonyms:
   a. imperious & intrinsic
   b. wan & pallid
   c. cabalistic & caper
   d. temporal & proximity

7. Pearl was dressed in a way that gave her a **similitude** to the scarlet letter:
   a. likeness
   b. a door, gate, or entrance
   c. still existing
   d. belonging to a thing by its very nature

8. The gardener had **relinquished** any idea of having the kind of garden
he had had in England:
   a. brought forward
   b. polished
   c. given up
   d. examined

9. Rev. Wilson had given public **reproof** of Hester in the marketplace:
   a. warm and pleasant words
   b. criticism; correction
   c. surrender
   d. assistance

10. A wide-ranging and impressive array or display is a:
    a. gauntlet
    b. eldritch
    c. muster
    d. panoply

11. Mr. Wilson asked Pearl what was wrong with her mother to **bedizen**
her in such a manner:
    a. dress gaudily or tastelessly
    b. correct
    c. beat with a whip
    d. instruct

12. They said they needed to take Pearl away for both her **temporal** and
eternal welfare:
    a. state of emergency
    b. nearness in place, time, etc.
    c. of or pertaining to time
    d. with it all

13. Rev. Dimmesdale was more **emaciated** than he had been three years
earlier:
    a. domineering
    b. weird
    c. pale
    d. abnormally thin

14. Gov. Bellingham said that Rev. Dimmesdale had **adduced** such
arguments that allowed things to remain as they were:
    a. polished
    b. brought forward
    c. argued
    d. divided

15. Pearl seemed to be "the **unpremeditated** offshoot of a passionate
moment:
    a. belonging by its nature
    b. banished; exiled
    c. not planned beforehand
    d. marked by great energy or vigor

16. Gov. Bellingham was dressed in the **antiquated** style of King James' reign:
    a. old fashioned; obsolete
    b. still existing
    c. elaborate in discourse or writing
    d. not imposing oneself on others

17. Rev. Dimmesdale was trembling with the **vehemence** of his appeal:
    a. morally corrupt
    b. impassioned; vigorous
    c. bold; not intimidated
    d. ghostly appearance

18. Hester felt she possessed **indefeasible** rights:
    a. containing occult meaning
    b. separated
    c. domineering
    d. not to be defeated

19. When Gov. Bellingham saw Pearl, he talked of the small **apparitions** he used to see in England at the Court-Masks:
    a. small children
    b. medicines
    c. ghosts; specters
    d. instructions

20. When Gov. Bellingham first entered, he was **expatiating** on his planned improvements:
    a. desiring to do good to others
    b. dictating
    c. giving correction
    d. elaborating in discourse

II.   **Matching: Place the letter of the correct answer in the blank:**

1.____ludicrous   A. still existing

2.____intrinsic   B. to form like a bow; arch; vault

3.____urchins   C. occupy a position at the flank or side

4.____pestilence   D. belonging to a thing by its very nature

5.____extant   E. a door, gate, or entrance

6.____cabalistic   F. a deadly or virulent epidemic disease

7.____caper   G. causing or deserving laughter; ridiculous

8.____flanked   H. to leap or skip in a sprightly manner

9.____portal   I. small boy or youngster

10.___embowed   J. containing an occult meaning

III.   **Matching: Place the letter of the correct answer in the blank:**

1.____tome   A. state of urgency or emergency

2.____burnished   B. the art or practice of medicine

3.____exigencies   C. instruction by question and answer

4.____genial   D. separate; part; divide

5.____benevolence   E. polished

6.____physic   F. a charlatan or quack who sells to an audience using tricks

7.____court mask   G. desire to do good to others

8.____catechism   H. a book, esp. a very heavy, large, or learned book

9.____mountebank   I. warmly and pleasantly cheerful

10.___sundering   J. masquerade party

ANSWERS TO VOCABULARY TEST CHAPTERS 7-8
THE SCARLET LETTER

I.   Multiple Choice:

1. c
2. a
3. d
4. d
5. c
6. b
7. a
8. c
9. b
10. d
11. a
12. c
13. d
14. b
15. c
16. a
17. b
18. d
19. c
20. d

II.   Matching:

1. G
2. D
3. I
4. F
5. A
6. J
7. H
8. C
9. E
10. B

III.   Matching:

1. H
2. E
3. A
4. I
5. G
6. B
7. J
8. C
9. F
10. D

VOCABULARY TEST CHAPTERS 9-11
THE SCARLET LETTER

I. Multiple Choice: Circle the letter of the correct answer:

1. Hester's husband was in Boston under a false **appellation**:
   a. necessity
   b. name
   c. period of watchful attention
   d. garment

2. Before Chillingworth came, the medical needs of the town were taken care of by a barber and an **apothecary**:
   a. an official of the church
   b. a medical student
   c. a druggist
   d. a veterinarian

3. Chillingworth had knowledge of the European **pharmacopoeia**:
   a. surgical instruments
   b. satanic concoctions
   c. illegal drugs
   d. a book containing a list of drugs

4. Rev. Dimmesdale's failing health was believed to be attributed to his **scrupulous** fulfillment of his duties as a pastor:
   a. rigorously precise or correct
   b. unfavorable; harmful
   c. overly urgent or persistent
   d. hard to understand

5. Rev. Dimmesdale began to keep **vigils**:
   a. oddities
   b. times of deep introspection
   c. periods of watchfulness at night
   d. present but not visible

6. The people of the town were **importunate** that Rev. Dimmesdale should take advantage of Chillingworth's skills:
   a. unfortunate
   b. begging earnestly
   c. joined together; united
   d. giving a false or misleading appearance

7. Roger Chillingworth **scrutinized** his patient:
   a. spoke ill of
   b. relieved without curing
   c. gave a false or misleading impression
   d. examined minutely

8. Rev. Dimmesdale moved in his library, which included works of monkish **erudition**:
    a. knowledge acquired by study
    b. causing sleep
    c. a stock of drugs
    d. oddities or peculiarities of conduct

9. Roger Chillingworth was a **diabolical** agent:
    a. hard to understand
    b. devilish; fiendish
    c. unfavorable
    d. not friendly

10. Chillingworth searched **stealthily**:
    a. in a short time
    b. placing between
    c. joined together
    d. secretly; escaping detection

11. Chillingworth said Pearl had to be allowed to live with her **eccentricities**:
    a. crafty schemes
    b. feelings of something happening
    c. oddities or peculiarities of conduct
    d. friendliness

12. Rev. Dimmesdale has been reading from a book of the **somniferous** school of literature:
    a. scholarly
    b. conforming to approved doctrine
    c. causing an increase in number
    d. causing sleep

13. Roger Chillingworth had a malice that had been **latent**:
    a. present but not visible
    b. not friendly
    c. devilish; fiendish
    d. unfavorable; harmful

14. Rev. Dimmesdale had feelings of **antipathy** toward Roger Chillingworth:
    a. agreement; harmony
    b. secretive
    c. friendliness
    d. a natural repugnance; aversion

15. Rev. Dimmesdale practiced constant **introspection** concerning his guilt:
    a. to make heavenly or celestial
    b. not giving a false appearance
    c. given to examine one's own thoughts
    d. crafty schemes or maneuvers

16. Although Rev. Dimmesdale and Roger Chillingworth exchanged views on philosophy, they returned to their views on what was **orthodox**:
    a. rigorously precise or correct
    b. conforming to approved doctrine
    c. joined together
    d. present but not visible

17. Roger Chillingworth had been **proffering** advice to Rev. Dimmesdale:
    a. speaking ill of
    b. sneaking up on
    c. feeling something bad is about to happen
    d. put before a person for acceptance

18. Rev. Dimmesdale thought his **presentiments** were part of his own imagination:
    a. feeling something bad will happen
    b. knowledge acquired by study
    c. oddities or peculiarities of conduct
    d. agreement between things

19. He had been given over to the **machinations** of his deadliest enemy:
    a. a natural repugnance; aversion
    b. crafty schemes or maneuvers
    c. something made by machinery
    d. something hidden

20. There were scholars who had acquired **abstruse** lore:
    a. devilish
    b. detestable
    c. necessary
    d. hard to understand

II.   Matching: Place the letter of the correct answer in the blank:

1.____vindicate   A. agreement between things; harmony

2.____chirurgical   B. capable of having the desired result or effect

3.____nether   C. unfavorable; harmful

4.____interposition   D. surgical

5.____concord   E. an official who maintains a church building

6.____vilified   F. to clear, as from an accusation or suspicion

7.____decried   G. the act of placing between

8.____efficacious   H. to speak ill of; defame; slander

9.____sexton   I. lying or believed to lie beneath the earth's surface; infernal

10.___inimical   J. denounced

III.   Matching: Place the letter of the correct answer in the blank:

1.____propagate   A. stopped short and stubbornly refused to go on

2.____burdock   B. made heavenly or celestial

3.____perforce   C. to relieve without curing

4.____conjoined   D. not giving a false or misleading appearance to

5.____anon   E. a coarse broad-leaved weed bearing prickly heads of burs

6.____palliate   F. in a short time; soon

7.____vestment   G. joined together; united

8.____balked   H. necessarily

9.____abhorrence   I. to cause to increase in number or amount

10.___etherealized   J. detestable; loathsome

11.___dissembled   K. garments worn by the clergy

ANSWERS TO VOCABULARY TEST CHAPTERS 9-11
THE SCARLET LETTER

I.   Multiple Choice:

1. b
2. c
3. d
4. a
5. c
6. b
7. d
8. a
9. b
10. d
11. c
12. d
13. a
14. d
15. c
16. b
17. d
18. a
19. b
20. d

II.   Matching:

1. F
2. D
3. I
4. G
5. A
6. H
7. J
8. B
9. E
10. C

III.   Matching:

1. I
2. E
3. H
4. G
5. F
6. C
7. K
8. A
9. J
10. B
11. D

VOCABULARY TEST CHAPTER 12
THE SCARLET LETTER

I. Multiple Choice: Circle the letter of the correct answer:

1. It was unclear whether or not Rev. Dimmesdale was suffering from **somnambulism**:
   a. selfishness; self-centeredness
   b. sleepwalking
   c. an incurable disease
   d. having regret for wrongdoing

2. The scaffold has seen many **culprits**:
   a. those who are unknown
   b. ghosts or specters
   c. persons guilty of crimes
   d. deadly or virulent diseases

3. Rev. Dimmesdale went to the scaffold in a vain attempt at **expiation**:
   a. ridicule; mockery
   b. to deal with lightly
   c. selfishness; self-centeredness
   d. atone for; make amends for

4. It is hard to know whether or not he went there in earnest or **mockery**:
   a. having regret for wrongdoing
   b. ridicule; derision
   c. of little or no importance
   d. grossly or obscenely abusive

5. Mr. Dimmesdale's scream had **multitudinous** echos:
   a. existing in great numbers; very numerous
   b. a violent and noisy commotion
   c. a loud uproar
   d. to increase in extent

6. Mr. Dimmesdale thought of some **defunct** transgressor:
   a. gruesome; horrible; revolting
   b. selfishness; self-centeredness
   c. no longer in existence
   d. stern

7. It was unsure whether or not Rev. Dimmesdale had a heart of **penitence**:
   a. selfishness; self-centeredness
   b. having regret for wrongdoing
   c. melancholy
   d. horror

8. Mistress Hibbins was known to make **excursions** into the forest to meet the Black Man at night:
   a. an indication of something about to happen
   b. loud uproars
   c. sleepwalking
   d. short trips or outings

9. The word that Hawthorne uses to refer to both to the light given off by the lantern, and the important person of Rev. Wilson is:
   a. luminary
   b. waxing
   c. multitudinous
   d. inextricable

10. Which of the two sets of words are synonyms:
    a. waxing and waning
    b. torrent and torpid
    c. askew and awry
    d. grimly and grisly

11. Rev. Dimmesdale had a thought that showed a **grisly** sense of humor:
    a. grossly or obscenely abusive
    b. causing a shudder or feeling of horror
    c. belonging to or seen in a vision
    d. no longer in existence

12. Rev. Dimmesale looked toward the **zenith** of the meteor:
    a. lowest point
    b. outer point
    c. inner point
    d. highest point

13. Because of his guilt, Rev. Dimmesdale had extended his **egotism** over the whole expanse of nature:
    a. selfishness; self-centeredness
    b. having regret for wrongdoing
    c. melancholy
    d. horror

14. Rev. Dimmesdale almost convinced himself he had seen the events of the night before as **visionary**:
    a. no longer in existence
    b. belonging to another time
    c. belonging or seen in a vision
    d. passing back and forth

15. The sexton returned his glove, **grimly** smiling:
    a. of little or no prominence or distinction
    b. causing a shudder or feeling of horror
    c. dealing with lightly
    d. sternly; harshly

16. The sexton said that the glove was on the scaffold because Satan had intended a **scurrilous** jest against Rev. Dimmesdale:
    a. grossly or obscenely abusive
    b. causing a shudder or feeling of horror
    c. belonging to or seen in a vision
    d. no longer in existence

17. The sexton spoke with Rev. Dimmesdale about the **portent** of the meteor the night before:
    a. belonging or seen in a vision
    b. of little or no prominence or distinction
    c. indication of something about to happen
    d. a body, object, etc. that give off light

18. Rev. Dimmesdale **conjectured** that Rev. Wilson had been praying at the deathbed of Gov. Winthrop:
    a. to speak ill of; defame
    b. to conclude from insufficient evidence
    c. to examine closely
    d. to observe from a distance

19. If Rev. Dimmesdale stood on the scaffold until he was unable to preach the next day, he would be **defrauding** his congregation:
    a. deprive of a right by fraud
    b. causing a shudder or feeling of horror
    c. ridiculing
    d. making amends for

20. As Pearl took his hand, Rev. Dimmesdale felt life pouring into him like a **torrent**:
    a. a violent and noisy commotion
    b. a loud uproar
    c. highest point
    d. a rushing, violent, abundant stream

II. **Matching: Place the letter of the correct answer in the blank:**

1.____obscure   A. increasing in extent

2.____catarrh   B. half inactive or sluggish

3.____trifled   C. inflammation of a mucous membrane, esp. of the
                          respiratory tract

4.____tumult   D. incapable of being disentangled

5.____waxing   E. dealt with lightly or without due seriousness

6.____inextricable   F. of little or no prominence or distinction

7.____half-torpid   G. a violent and noisy commotion

ANSWERS TO VOCABULARY TEST CHAPTER 12
THE SCARLET LETTER

I. Multiple Choice:

1. b
2. c
3. d
4. b
5. a
6. c
7. b
8. d
9. a
10. c
11. b
12. d
13. a
14. c
15. d
16. a
17. c
18. b
19. a
20. d

II. Matching:

1. F
2. C
3. E
4. G
5. A
6. D
7. B

VOCABULARY TEST CHAPTERS 13-14
THE SCARLET LETTER

I.   Multiple Choice: Circle the letter of the correct answer:

1. After seeing Rev. Dimmesdale on the scaffold at midnight, Hester realized that "his moral force was **abased** into more than childish weakness:
    a. bestowed as a gift
    b. set free
    c. stirred up
    d. humiliated; degraded

2. The scarlet letter glittered with its **fantastic** embroidery:
    a. prosperous; fortunate
    b. extravagantly fanciful; lavish
    c. shockingly frightful
    d. conspicuous

3. Because of her scarlet letter, Hester became a person of **prominence** before the community:
    a. conspicuous
    b. prosperous; fortunate
    c. suited to the purpose or occasion
    d. outward aspect or appearance

4. In the matter of Hester Prynne there was neither irritation nor **irksomeness**:
    a. determination
    b. shockingly frightful
    c. annoying; irritating
    d. stirred up

5. When Hester gave of what she had to the needy, they returned her kindness with a **gibe**:
    a. reward
    b. insulting remark
    c. a feeling of future evil
    d. a purpose or intention

6. People stopped interpreting the scarlet letter by its original **signification**:
    a. talking; conversing
    b. a natural tendency or inclination
    c. purpose or intention
    d. meaning; import; sense

7. If people were **resolute** to stop Hester in the street, she would lay her finger on the scarlet letter:
   a. determined; firmly set in purpose
   b. dangerous
   c. obstructed; hindered
   d. to see; recognize

8. The public is **despotic** in temperament:
   a. determined; firmly set in purpose
   b. stirred up
   c. tyrannical; oppressive
   d. forceful

9. Society was inclined to show Hester a more **benign** countenance than she wanted:
   a. dangerous
   b. of kindly disposition
   c. humiliated
   d. shockingly frightful

10. The **propensity** of human nature is to tell the worst of itself:
    a. determined; firmly set in purpose
    b. shockingly frightful
    c. a natural tendency or inclination
    d. of kindly disposition

11. Human nature **constrains** them to whisper one black scandal of bygone years:
    a. bestow as a gift
    b. seize and hold by force without legal right
    c. command
    d. to force, compel or oblige

12. Hester Prynne assumed a freedom of **speculation**:
    a. contemplation or consideration
    b. outward aspect or appearance
    c. set with some mark of disgrace or infamy
    d. nearness in time and place

13. Thoughts visited her that would have been considered as **perilous** as demons to their entertainer:
    a. nearness in time and place
    b. dangerous
    c. stirred up
    d. broken; incomplete

14. Pearl was the **effluence** of her mother's lawless passion:
    a. tranquility; peacefulness
    b. meaning; import; sense
    c. something that flows out
    d. a person that ruins or spoils

15. Hester knew that Dimmesdale had a secret enemy who was dwelling with him under the **semblance** of a friend:
    a. outward aspect or appearance
    b. tranquility; peacefulness
    c. natural tendency or inclination
    d. purpose or intention

16. Pearl's reflection had a **fragmentary** smile:
    a. ridiculing; mocking
    b. broken; incomplete
    c. a deep gap or break
    d. of kindly disposition; gracious

17. Roger Chillingworth told Hester that the magistrates had been **discoursing** about her affairs:
    a. set free
    b. submit or comply without protest
    c. have a feeling of future evil
    d. talking; conversing

18. An expression flickered over Chillingworth's face **derisively**:
    a. conspicuously
    b. ridiculing; mocking
    c. dangerously
    d. determined; firmly set in purpose

19. Hester reminded Chillingworth of his previous conversation in which he **extorted** her promise to keep his identity secret:
    a. obtained by force or threat
    b. contemplated or considered
    c. bestowed as a gift
    d. submit or comply without protest

20. Chillingworth said that he had taken his revenge by his constant **propinquity** to the man who had wronged him:
    a. ridiculing; mocking
    b. stirred up
    c. have a feeling of future evil
    d. nearness in time and place

II. Matching: Place the letter of the correct answer in the blank:

1.____groveled   A. set with some mark of disgrace or infamy

2.____apt   B. have a feeling of future evil

3.____meed   C. a cliff with a vertical or overhanging face

4.____stigmatized   D. prosperous; fortunate

5.____quietude   E. reward

6.____precipice   F. a deep gap or break

7.____chasm   G. suited to the occasion or purpose

8.____ghastly   H. tranquility; peacefulness

9.____foreboded   I. lie or fall with the face down and the body prostrate

10.___auspicious   J. shockingly frightful or dreadful; horrible

III. Matching: Place the letter of the correct answer in the blank:

1.____acquiescing   A. a purpose or intention

2.____agitated   B. to take vengeance on

3.____purport   C. a person or thing that ruins or spoils

4.____behest   D. stirred up

5.____peradventure   E. a command; directive

6.____avenged   F. submit or comply without protest

7.____discern   G. chance, doubt, uncertainty

8.____bane   H. to see; recognize

ANSWERS TO VOCABULARY CHAPTERS 13-14
THE SCARLET LETTER

I.   Multiple Choice:

1. d
2. b
3. a
4. c
5. b
6. d
7. a
8. c
9. b
10. c
11. d
12. a
13. b
14. d
15. a
16. b
17. d
18. b
19. a
20. d

II.   Matching:

1. I
2. G
3. E
4. A
5. H
6. C
7. F
8. J
9. B
10. D

III. Matching:

1. F
2. D
3. A
4. E
5. G
6. B
7. H
8. C

VOCABULARY TEST CHAPTERS 15-16
THE SCARLET LETTER

I. **Multiple Choice: Circle the letter of the correct answer:**

1. Hester watched Chillingworth, wondering if the grass would be **blighted** where he has walked:
   a. green
   b. sharply stinging or bitter
   c. animated; spirited
   d. deteriorated or ruined

2. Chillingworth was very **sedulous** in his gathering of herbs:
   a. taking great pleasure
   b. diligent; persevering
   c. harshness or sharpness
   d. charged with a fault

3. Hester wondered if the vegetation would be changed into something **deleterious** by his touch:
   a. injurious to health
   b. sharply stinging or bitter
   c. not able to be felt
   d. green

4. Hester wondered if there was an **ominous** shadow following Chillingworth:
   a. to become wrecked; fail utterly
   b. existing in one from birth
   c. sharpness
   d. portending evil or harm

5. She remembered when he would study in the light of her **nuptial** smile:
   a. existing in one from birth
   b. a puzzling occurrence or situation
   c. of or pertaining to marriage
   d. animated; spirited

6. She considered it a crime that she had ever **reciprocated** his lukewarm affection:
   a. chattered or babbled
   b. to give or feel in return
   c. showing sudden irritation
   d. to be animated; witty; sparkling

7. Most of Pearl's ships **foundered** near the shore:
   a. to become wrecked; fail utterly
   b. to be animate
   c. to take great pleasure in
   d; witty; sparkling

8. Which of the following does **not** belong:
   a. listlessness
   b. scintillating
   c. despondency
   d. haggard

9. Pearl, born as a result of her parents' breaking of God's moral law, was a child who was lawless, disobedient and difficult to control. Which of the following does **not** describe her character:
   a. waywardness
   b. capricious
   c. petulant
   d. beneficence

10. Hester thought Pearl's **precocity** might make her a suitable friend:
    a. open or unqualified contempt
    b. talkativeness
    c. unusually advanced or mature
    d. showing little interest in anything

11. Pearl had always hovered about the **enigma** of the scarlet letter:
    a. the extreme limit
    b. a puzzling occurrence or situation
    c. harshness or sharpness of tone
    d. a small, usually wooded valley

12. Hester told Pearl with **asperity** that she would put her into a dark closet if she did not stop asking the same question:
    a. harshness or sharpness of tone
    b. disobedience
    c. talkativeness
    d. the extreme limit

13. Hester knew she had to tell Rev. Dimmesdale the truth, even if there were **ulterior** consequences:
    a. showing little interest in anything
    b. thoughtfulness or sadness
    c. doing good or causing good
    d. intentionally kept concealed

14. Hester and Pearl walked into the **primeval** forest:
    a. injurious to health
    b. of or pertaining to the first age
    c. portending evil or harm
    d. the extreme limit

15. The brook continued in its never ceasing **loquacity**:
    a. animated; spirited
    b. yearning for something
    c. talkativeness
    d. small whirlpools

16. Pearl tried to mingle her lighter **cadence** with the melancholy song of the brook:
    a. beat, rate, or measure of rhythm
    b. yearning for something
    c. talkativeness
    d. small whirlpools

17. Maybe the brook was making a prophetic **lamentation** about something that had not yet happened:
    a. chatter or babble
    b. expression of grief
    c. feeling or showing profound hopelessness

18. Pearl chose to break off her acquaintance with the **repining** brook:
    a. chatter or babble
    b. expression of grief
    c. yearning for something
    d. instances of misbehavior

19. When Rev. Dimmesdale came into view, he was looking **haggard** and feeble:
    a. charged with a fault
    b. gaunt, wasted, exhausted
    c. animated; spirited
    d. showing sudden irritation

20. When Pearl associated the scarlet letter with the minister's hand over his heart, at first Hester smiled at the **incongruity** of that thought:
    a. inconsistent
    b. pictured
    c. inclined to cause harm
    d. portending great evil or harm

II. Matching: Place the letter of the correct answer in the blank:

1.____sere   A. instances of misbehaviors

2.____verdure   B. not able to be felt

3.____malignant   C. open or unqualified contempt

4.____bask   D. greenness

5.____impalpable   E. to take great pleasure in

6.____dexterity   F. sharpness

7.____hornbook   G. skill using the hands

8.____misdemeanors   H. inclined to cause harm, suffering or distress

9.____acuteness   I. withered

10.___scorn   J. a primer formerly used in teaching children to read

III. Matching: Place the letter of the correct answer in the blank:

1.____acrid   A. existing in one from birth

2.____innate   B. before

3.____imputed   C. a disease with tumors of the neck, chin, armpits, etc.

4.____whither   D. about to happen

5.____betimes   E. sharply stinging and bitter

6.____imaged   F. a small, usually wooded valley

7.____extremity   G. charged with a fault

8.____scrofula   H. pictured; imagined

9.____dell   I. to what place; where

10.___impending   J. the extreme limit

ANSWERS TO VOCABULARY TEST CHAPTERS 15-16
THE SCARLET LETTER

I.   Multiple Choice:

1. d
2. b
3. a
4. d
5. c
6. b
7. a
8. b
9. d
10. c
11. b
12. a
13. d
14. b
15. c
16. a
17. b
18. c
19. b
20. a

II.   Matching:

1. I
2. D
3. H
4. E
5. B
6. G
7. J
8. A
9. F
10. C

III.   Matching:

1. E
2. A
3. G
4. I
5. B
6. H
7. C
8. F
9. D

VOCABULARY TESTS CHAPTERS 17-19
THE SCARLET LETTER

I. Multiple Choice: Circle the letter of the correct answer:

1. Arthur and Hester felt they were observing **disembodied** beings:
   a. inhabitants; residents
   b. provoking expectation, interest, or desire
   c. souls without bodies
   d. a change in outward form or appearance

2. The two had long been **estranged** by the circumstances of their lives:
   a. kept at a distance; alienated
   b. marked by great vigor or energy
   c. causing grief or great sorrow
   d. wearing away by irritation

3. Hester knew that Arthur had been at the mercy of one whose motives were **malevolent**:
   a. freedom from narrow restrictions
   b. not to be revoked or recalled
   c. attentive to the smallest detail
   d. wishing evil or harm on others

4. The very **contiguity** of his enemy made him more dangerous:
   a. kept at a distance; alienated
   b. provoking expectation, interest, or desire
   c. touching; in contact
   d. brought under control; mastered

5. It is possible that Hester had left the minister to bear his problems because of the **misanthropy** of her own:
   a. freedom from narrow restrictions
   b. hatred of mankind
   c. causing grief or great sorrow
   d. wearing away by irritation

6. Hester watched Arthur undergo a dark **transfiguration**:
   a. a change in outward form or appearance
   b. changing from one nature to another
   c. offense to decency
   d. soften in feeling or temper; pacify

7. The **indelicacy** of exposing his guilty heart to the one who would gloat over it:
   a. easily angered
   b. causing grief or great sorrow
   c. corrupted
   d. offensive to decency

8. Arthur answered out of an **abyss** of sadness:
    a. a fortress
    b. a system of writing consisting of pictures
    c. a bottomless pit
    d. a stain or reproach on one's reputation

9. Hester said she thought Cillingworth would find other ways of
    satiating his dark passions:
    a. wearing away by irritation
    b. satisfying to the full
    c. atoning for; making amends for
    d. to hinder, hamper, burden

10. Hester had **habituated** herself to spending time with only her
    thoughts:
    a. to accustom to a particular situation
    b. to place between
    c. to be unable to avoid
    d. to decorate

11. Hester had a certain **latitude** of speculation:
    a. brought under control
    b. provoking expectation, interest, or desire
    c. violated a law; sinned
    d. freedom from narrow restrictions

12. The minister had **transgressed** one of the most sacred of the laws:
    a. to accustom to a particular situation
    b. kept at a distance; alienated
    c. violated a law; sinned
    d. make seem less serious by offering excuses

13. If a man like Rev. Dimmesdale were to fall into sin again, what plea
    could be made in **extenuation**:
    a. comfort
    b. make seem less serious by offering excuses
    c. not to be recalled or revoked
    d. brought under control; mastered

14. He had been broken down by **exquisite** suffering:
    a. restrained
    b. unable to be avoided
    c. toughened or hardened by use
    d. intense; acute

15. Taking off the scarlet letter had an **exhilarating** effect on Hester:
    a. invigorating
    b. atoning for; making amends
    c. restraining
    d. wearing away by irritation

16. When the **stigma** was gone, Hester sighed in relief:
    a. a nymph of the woods
    b. a fortress
    c. a stain or reproach on one's reputation
    d. a load

17. The sunshine was **transmuting** the yellow fallen leaves to gold:
    a. a change in outward form or appearance
    b. changing from one nature to another
    c. offense to decency
    d. soften in feeling or temper; pacify

18. The nature of the forest was never **subjugated** by human law:
    a. easily angered
    b. restrained
    c. not to be revoked or recalled
    d. brought under control; mastered

19. The small **denizens** of the wilderness hardly bothered to move out of Pearl's path:
    a. nymphs of the woods
    b. persons of despicable character
    c. inhabitants; residents
    d. demons

20. The squirrel is a **choleric** little personage:
    a. easily angered
    b. restrained
    c. not to be revoked or recalled
    d. brought under control; mastered

21. Pearl was a living **hieroglyphic**:
    a. visually charming or quaint
    b. a system of writing consisting of pictures
    c. combination of mental & emotional traits
    d. a stain or reproach on one's reputation

22. Hester felt in some indistinct and **tantalizing** manner estranged from Pearl:
    a. brought under control
    b. provoking expectation, interest, or desire
    c. violated a law; sinned
    d. freedom from narrow restrictions

23. Hester was **inured** to Pearl's behavior at other times:
    a. toughened or hardened by use or exposure
    b. corrupted
    c. softened in feeling or temper; pacify
    d. unable to be avoided

24. Pearl was not at all **mollified** by her mother:
    a. toughened or hardened by use or exposure
    b. corrupted
    c. softened in feeling or temper; pacify
    d. unable to be avoided

25. Pearl was **gesticulating** wildly:
    a. drawing out of shape
    b. use gestures in an animated or exited way
    c. provoking expectation, interest, or desire
    d. changing from one nature to another

II. Matching: Place the letter of the correct answer in the blank:

1.___devoid   A. attentive to the smallest details

2.___wretch   B. causing grief or great sorrow

3.___grievous   C. wearing away by irritation

4.___striven   D. without

5.___dolefully   E. hinder; hamper; burden

6.___cumber   F. struggled vigorously

7.___colloquy   G. a person of despicable or base character

8.___minuteness   H. sorrowfully

9.___trammeled   I. a conversational exchange; conference

10._fretting   J. restrained

II. Matching: Place the letter of the correct answer in the blank:

1.____expiating   A. combination of mental and emotional traits

2.____citadel   B. drawing out of shape

3.____temperament   C. unable to avoid

4.____adorn   D. a nymph of the woods

5.____dryad   E. a fortress

6.____picturesqueness   F. corrupted

7.____entreaties   G. decorate

8.____contortions   H. visually charming or quaint

9.____cankered   I. atoning for; making amends for

10.___inevitable   J. earnest requests; pleas

ANSWERS TO VOCABULARY TEST CHAPTERS 17-19
THE SCARLET LETTER

I. Multiple Choice:

1. c
2. a
3. d
4. c
5. b
6. a
7. d
8. c
9. b
10. a
11. d
12. c
13. b
14. d
15. a
16. c
17. b
18. d
19. c
20. a
21. b
22. b
23. a
24. c
25. b

II. Matching:

1. D
2. G
3. B
4. F
5. H
6. E
7. I
8. A
9. J
10. C

III.   Matching:

    1. I
    2. E
    3. A
    4. G
    5. D
    6. H
    7. J
    8. B
    9. F
    10. C

VOCABULARY TEST CHAPTERS 20-24
THE SCARLET LETTER

I.   Multiple Choice: Circle the letter of the correct Choice:

1. As Rev. Dimmesdale left the forest, he felt that such a great **vicissitude** in his life could not be received as real:
   a. something remarkable or extraordinary
   b. change of one state or thing to another
   c. sorrow for wrongdoing
   d. lack of energy

2. Which of the following does **not** refer to an entertainer:
   a. gleeman
   b. minstrel
   c. Merry Andrew
   d. jocularity

3. In order to free his mind from the **duplicity** of impression which vexed it:
   a. subject to change
   b. deceitfulness
   c. great quantity
   d. incapable of being tired out

4. Rev. Dimmesdale was considered to be an **exemplary** man:
   a. rude, uncivil, boorish
   b. showing enthusiasm, excitement, liveliness
   c. subject to change
   d. commendable

5. As Rev. Dimmesdale entered the town, there was a **phenomenon** which made him feel that everything was different:
   a. something remarkable or extraordinary
   b. not restrained by morals; unprincipled
   c. something of little value
   d. moral or ethical consideration

6. With each step he was **incited** to do some strange, wild, or wicked thing:
   a. directed outward from the center
   b. to keep down or suppress
   c. made; caused to be
   d. stimulated to action

7. He could hardly keep himself from whispering some **blasphemous** suggestion:
   a. rude; unmannerly
   b. not to be disputed or contested
   c. speak irreverently of God
   d. affected an angry expression

8. He could hardly keep from laughing when he thought of how the **sanctified** old patriarch would have reacted:
   a. serious
   b. to make holy
   c. deified; glorified
   d. lasting only a short time

9. Rev. Dimmedale had convinced the young woman to exchange the **transitory** pleasures of the world for a heavenly hope:
   a. lasting a short time
   b. working or acting merely for money
   c. being without cause or justification
   d. characterized by joking

10. The young woman **ransacked** her conscience:
    a. to pay or give compensation for
    b. filled with horror or fear
    c. directed outward from the center
    d. searched thoroughly and vigorously

11. There were **dissolute** sailors present in the town:
    a. irritated; annoyed
    b. indifferent to moral restraints; immoral
    c. brisk; active
    d. incapable of being tired out

12. Rev. Dimmesdale told Mistress Hibbins he did not go into the forest seeking a **potentate**:
    a. an unfavorable or critical comment
    b. bold, reckless outlaw
    c. person possessing great power
    d. one who practices divination

13. When Rev. Dimmesdale returned to his apartment, he ate with a **ravenous** appetite:
    a. extremely hungry
    b. stormy; turbulent
    c. unusual
    d. very weak

14. Pearl's "**effervescence** made her flit with birdlike movement:"
    a. expressing sorrow or melancholy
    b. showing enthusiasm, excitement, liveliness
    c. not restrained by morals; unprincipled
    d. stormy; turbulent

15. The sailors were rough looking **desperadoes**:
    a. those who work merely for money
    b. persons possessing great power
    c. future generations
    d. bold, reckless outlaws

16. Which of the following does **not** refer to a kind of medicine:
    a. cordial
    b. wormwood
    c. scurvy
    d. aloes

17. The sailors were only subject to the law of a **tempestuous** wind:
    a. stormy; turbulent
    b. lasting only a short time
    c. directed outward from the center
    d. moving in a wave-like motion

18. There was no **animadversion** when someone like Roger Chillingworth was seen talking to the ship's captain:
    a. bewilderment
    b. integrity and uprightness; honesty
    c. an unfavorable or critical remark
    d. harmonious combination of elements

19. They heard the sound of military music approaching along a **contiguous** street:
    a. to be on top or above
    b. brilliantly clear
    c. subject to change
    d. touching; in contact

20. The early statesmen had **fortitude** and self-reliance:
    a. not restrained by morals; unprincipled
    b. mental and emotional strength
    c. working or acting merely for money
    d. lack of energy

21. Rev. Dimmesdale was a young and eminently distinguished **divine**:
    a. a priest or cleric
    b. one who listens
    c. one who practices divination
    d. person possessing great power

22. As the procession moved along, Rev. Dimmesdale's look was so **abstracted** it was doubtful he even heard the music:
    a. indicated or made known indirectly
    b. expressing sorrow or melancholy
    c. thought of apart from concrete reality
    d. the state of being complete

23. Mistress Hibbins was considered to be one who participated in **necromancy**:
    a. uncompromised honesty
    b. divination through invocation of the dead
    c. inclined or disposed to war
    d. state of being seen by the eye

24. As Pearl danced among the participants, her energy was doubly **indefatigable**:
    a. incapable of being tired out
    b. too deep to understand
    c. lacking vigor or vitality
    d. shameless boldness

25. Pearl approached the Indians with **audacity**:
    a. subject to change
    b. shameless boldness
    c. filled with horror or fear
    d. bewilderment

II. Matching: Antonyms: Place the letter of the antonym in the blank:

1.____uncouth   A. repose

2.____effervescence   B. decorum

3.____inducements   C. unscrupulous

4.__tempestuous   D. disreuptable

5.____integrity   E. impediments

6.____probity   F. languor

III. Matching: Place the letter of the correct answer in the blank:

1.____antiquity   A. brisk; active

2.____apprehend   B. having a disposition to impose oneself on others

3.____obtrusive   C. future generations

4.____unwonted   D. property/funds furnished to a person or institution

5.____posterity   E. strong alcoholic liquor

6.____ferocity   F. ancient times

7.____aquavitae   G. unusual

8.____profusion   H. understand

9.____galliard   I. savagely fierce or cruel

10.___endowments   J. great quantity

IV. Matching: Place the letter of the correct answer in the blank:

1.____surmounted

2.____consternation

3.____clarion

4.____compeers

5.____aspiring

6.____stomacher

7.____trifle

8.____orb

9.____oracles

10.___symphonious

11.___apotheosized

12.___appalled

13.___nugatory

14.___bequeathed

15.___armorial

A. sphere or globe

B. deified; glorified

C. longing, aiming, or seeking ambitiously

D. pertaining to a coat of arms

E. sudden, alarming amazement or dread resulting in confusion

F. to be on top or above

G. filled with horror or fear

H. associates; equals

I. something of little value, importance, or consequence

J. brilliantly clear

K. disposed of property in a will

L. those who deliver authoritative & influential pronouncements

M. a harmonious combination of elements

N. an ornament or support for the breast, worn by females

O. trifling or worthless

ANSWERS TO VOCABULARY TEST CHAPTERS 20-24
THE SCARLET LETTER

I.   Multiple Choice:

1. b
2. d
3. b
4. d
5. a
6. d
7. c
8. b
9. a
10. d
11. b
12. c
13. a
14. b
15. d
16. c
17. a
18. c
19. d
20. b
21. a
22. c
23. b
24. a
25. b

II.   Matching: Antonyms:

1. B
2. F
3. E
4. A
5. C
6. D

III.   Matching:

1. F
2. H
3. B
4. G
5. C
6. I
7. E
8. J
9. A
10. D

IV.   Matching:

1. F
2. E
3. J
4. H
5. C
6. N
7. I
8. A
9. L
10. M
11. B
12. G
13. O
14. K
15. D

THE SCARLET LETTER TEST

I.   **Multiple Choice: Circle the letter of the correct choice:**

1. The setting of *The Scarlet Letter* is:
   a. 18th century England
   b. 17th century England
   c. 18th century Boston
   d. 17th century Boston

2. At the time when Hester Prynne lived, the normal punishment for adultery was:
   a. imprisonment
   b. death
   c. wearing a scarlet letter
   d. exile

3. Hester was told that, in order to save her soul, she must:
   a. repent & turn from her sin
   b. repent & reveal the baby's father
   c. do good works
   d. confess her sin in public

4. Hester's husband tells her she should tell him who the baby's father is because:
   a. he has hurt them both
   b. he plans to kill him
   c. she owes it to him
   d. she'll be sorry if she doesn't

5. Hester named her child Pearl because:
   a. she was such a placid child
   b. it was Hester's favorite name
   c. she had smooth, white skin
   d. she was a treasure, bought with a great price

6. Hester's child is:
   a. obedient & even tempered
   b. unruly & has temper tantrums
   c. pleasant & friendly
   d. like other children her age

7. When the people of the town decided that Pearl should be taken from Hester, to whom did she appeal to help to argue her case:
   a. Roger Chillingworth
   b. Gov. Bellingham
   c. Rev. Wilson
   d. Rev. Dimmesdale

8. When Rev. Dimmesdale stood on the scaffold it was:
   a. noon
   b. midnight
   c. early morning
   d. afternoon

9. Mr. Dimmesdale had a "great horror of mind" believing the whole universe could see:
   a. his weakened condition
   b. his insanity
   c. his guilt
   d. the red mark over his heart

10. Dimmesdale tells Pearl he will publicly stand with her and her mother:
    a. the next day
    b. in a month
    c. before the judgment seat
    d. when he is well

11. The plot of *The Scarlet Letter* is mainly concerned with:
    a. Hester & Dimmesdale's relationship
    b. how Hester fell into sin
    c. the results of sin
    d. how Hester was saved

12. The climax that occurs in Chapter 12 is:
    a. Dimmesdale's sin being revealed
    b. Hester, Pearl & Dimmesdale join hands
    c. Hester's sin being revealed
    d. Pearl being told who her father is

13. Hester's view of salvation was false because:
    a. she did not believe in salvation
    b. she put her trust in her abilities
    c. she put her faith in God
    d. none of the above

14. The way Hester felt about Chillingworth was:
    a. she loved him
    b. she hated him
    c. she pitied him
    d. she feared him

15. Pearl associated her mother's scarlet letter with:
    a. sin
    b. the minister's hand over his heart
    c. beauty
    d. sunshine

16. Hester told Pearl she wore the scarlet letter:
    a. because of her shame
    b. because of its beauty
    c. because it was the law
    d. because of the gold thread

17. Hester resolved to reveal to Dimmesdale:
    a. her past
    b. her need for him
    c. Chillingworth's true character
    d. the town gossip

18. When Hester met Dimmesdale in the forest, the setting was significant because:
    a. they went there often
    b. it signified Hester's moral weakness
    c. she could be herself there
    d. it was Pearl's favorite place

19. Pearl asked her mother why Dimmesdale did not:
    a. live with them
    b. leave town
    c. wear a scarlet letter
    d. wear the Black Man's mark on the outside of his bosom

20. Dimmesdale's life had been more painful than Hester's because:
    a. he was living a lie
    b. he was supposed to be a spiritual leader
    c. he was covering up sin
    d. all of the above

21. When Dimmesdale heard Chillingworth's true identity, he first said that:
    a. he could not forgive Hester
    b. he would kill himself
    c. he forgave Hester immediately
    d. he would kill Chillingworth

22. Hester advised Dimmesdale to:
    a. confess before the townspeople
    b. keep things the way they were
    c. run away to Europe
    d. none of the above

23. In the woods, Hester:
    a. took off the scarlet letter
    b. covered up the scarlet letter
    d. none of the above

24. When Dimmesdale left the forest, he was:
    a. weak and barely able to walk
    b. suffering and in pain
    c. strong and energetic
    d. sad and lonely

25. Because of the decision he and Hester had made in the forest, Dimmesdale returned to town and felt:
    a. strongly tempted to do evil
    b. tremendous relief
    c. absolved of all guilt
    d. grateful to God for what He had done

26. When Dimmesdale marched in the procession on Election Day, he was:
    a. weak and in pain
    b. energetic and strong
    c. looking at Hester & Pearl
    d. sad and lonely

27. After Dimmesdale preached, people thought that he was:
    a. getting better and stronger
    b. looking weaker
    c. going to leave the town
    d. going to die & go to heaven

28. Dimmesdale died after:
    a. making a public confession of his sin
    b. pledging his love to Hester & Pearl
    c. a private time of confession
    d. apologizing to Chillingworth

29. People said that Dimmesdale's scarlet letter was the result of:
    a. self inflicted torture
    b. Dimmesdale's remorse
    c. Chillingworth's magic & drugs
    d. all of the above

30. After Rev. Dimmesdale's death, Roger Chillingworth:
    a. repented of his sins
    b. withered up without revenge & died
    c. lived in Boston for 10 years
    d. moved back to Europe

II.   Matching: Place the letter of the correct answer in the blank:

1._____rose   A. metaphor & simile used by Hawthorne to refer to Pearl

2._____Pearl   B. thought to be the letter A in the sky

3._____wild bird   C. What Hester says Chillingworth has been transformed into

4._____kiss   D. a "conjunction" between Hester & Dimmesdale

5._____Hester   E. what the letter A came to represent

6._____Dimmesdale F. Hawthorne's symbol of love & hope

7._____meteor   G. has meaning on more than one level

8._____able   H. on the verge of lunacy

9._____symbol   I. Pearl tried to wash this off

10._____fiend   J. would not go to Dimmesdale in his study for fear of scandal

III.   True/False: Write T or F in the blank:

1._____ When Hester went to the governor's palace to deliver gloves & plead for custody of Pearl, Hester said she would die without Pearl.

2._____ When she arrived at the governor's palace, she found the governor, Rev. Mather, Rev. Dimmesdale and Roger Chillingworth there.

3._____ Pearl was friendly with all of the men present.

4._____ Pearl was a homely child of average intelligence.

5._____ The people of Boston believed Pearl resembled a living scarlet letter.

6._____ In *The Scarlet Letter*, the character who represented satanic dealings and witchcraft was Pearl.

7._____ Roger Chillingworth is called the leech.

8._____ Pearl asked her mother what the scarlet letter meant.

9._____ The climax is the end of a literary work.

10._____Dimmesdale was going to go assume a new identity and work among the Indians.

IV.   Short answer: Choose 5 to answer:

1.   What advantage did Chillingworth have over Dimmesdale?

2.   Explain the statement, "The scarlet letter had not done its office."

3.   What lie did Hester tell to Pearl?

4.   What was the story Pearl had heard from Mistress Hibbins?

5.   When they were in the woods, what action of Hester caused Pearl to throw a temper tantrum?

6.   How did children usually respond to Arthur Dimmesdale?

ANSWERS TO THE SCARLET LETTER TEST

I. Multiple Choice:

1. d
2. b
3. b
4. a
5. d
6. b
7. d
8. b
9. d
10. c
11. c
12. b
13. b
14. b
15. b
16. d
17. c
18. b
19. d
20. d
21. a
22. c
23. a
24. c
25. a
26. b
27. d
28. a
29. d
30. b

II.   Matching:

1. F
2. D
3. A
4. I
5. J
6. H
7. B
8. E
9. G
10. C

III.   True/False:

1. T
2. F
3. F
4. F
5. T
6. F
7. T
8. T
9. F
10. F

IV.   Short Answer:

See answers to individual chapter questions.

Scarlet Letter Vocab Ch 1-3A

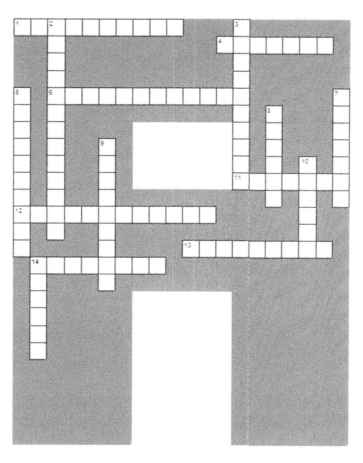

Across

1. tombs; graves; burial places
4. an idle person without visible means of support
6. unfavorable
11. a building
12. having prominent brows
13. signified by some visible object
14. a court of justice

Down

2. faces
3. a civil officer charged with the administration of the law
5. without changing
7. to divine or predict
8. an ideal place or state
9. of great weight. heavy; massive
10. moral excellence
14. crowd

Scarlet Letter Vocab Ch 1-3A

Across

1. tombs; graves; burial places
4. an idle person without visible means of support
6. unfavorable
11. a building
12. having prominent brows
13. signified by some visible object
14. a court of justice

Down

2. faces
3. a civil officer charged with the administration of the law
5. without changing
7. to divine or predict
8. an ideal place or state
9. of great weight; heavy; massive
10. moral excellence
14. crowd

Scarlet Letter Vocab Ch 1-3B

Across

2. sinner
7. a brazen or disreputable woman
11. conduct; behavior; facial appearance
12. to believe, trust, think, or suppose
13. a messenger or crier of the court

Down

1. a female person who violates the law
3. make embarrassed or ashamed
4. a raised platform or stage
5. full toned or sonorous
6. to purpose or intention
8. extremely bad reputation; public reproach; strong condemnation as a result of a shameful act
9. decorations or embellishments
10. the quality or condition of being improper

Scarlet Letter Vocab Ch 1-3B

Across

2. sinner
7. a brazen or disreputable woman
11. conduct, behavior, facial appearance
12. to believe, trust, think, or suppose
13. a messenger or crier of the court

Down

1. a female person who violates the law
3. make embarrassed or ashamed
4. a raised platform or stage
5. full toned or sonorous
6. to purpose or intention
8. extremely bad reputation; public reproach; strong condemnation as a result of a shameful act
9. decorations or embellishments
10. the quality or condition of being improper

Scarlet Letter Vocab Ch 1-3C

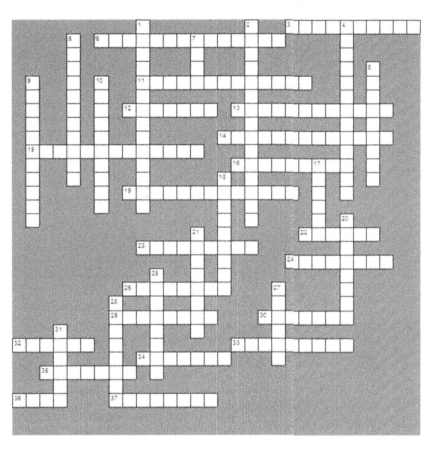

Across

3 conduct, behavior
6 optical illusions in which figures increase or diminish in size, pass into each other, etc
11 mental impressions retained and revived
12 a temporary stay
13 lack of interest or concern
14 composed of parts of different kinds
15 very slight or subtle
16 characterized by trembling, as from fear, nervousness, or weakness
19 without or not subject to a particular feeling or sensation
22 appearance to the eye or mind
23 skilled in fluent, forceful and appropriate speech
24 make wrinkles in the face
26 personal disgrace, dishonor
29 added as a supplement
30 continues to irritate or cause bitter resentment
32 the face, usually with reference to shape features, expression
33 to threaten, menace
34 disdainfully proud, snobbish, arrogant
35 wooden framework with holes for securing head and hands, used to expose offender to public derision
36 accustomed to, used to
37 having or showing acute mental discernment, shrewd

Down

1 involving one within another
2 exceptional or abnormal
4 without regret for wrongdoing
5 the quality or condition of being improper
7 being or demeanor
8 a formal discussion of a subject in speech or written talk, as a sermon
9 a hoop petticoat, or circles of hoops used to extend the petticoat
10 gloomy state of mind
17 eyes
18 stubbornness
20 spiteful; malignant
21 to become quiet, less active
25 hellish; diabolical, fiendish
27 boldly shameless
28 a shafted weapon with an axlike cutting blade, beak and spike
31 Roman Catholic

Scarlet Letter Vocab Ch 1-3C

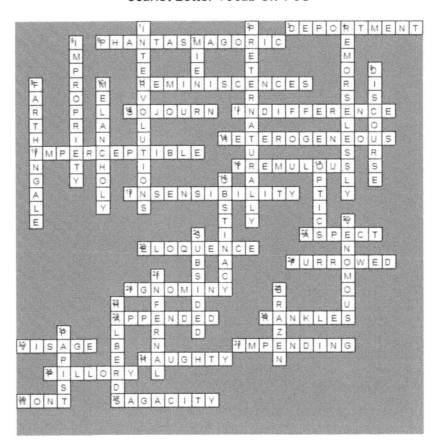

Across

3. conduct, behavior
6. optical illusions in which figures increase or diminish in size, pass into each other, etc.
11. mental impressions retained and revived
12. a temporary stay
13. lack of interest or concern
14. composed of parts of different kinds
15. very slight or subtle
16. characterized by trembling, as from fear, nervousness, or weakness
19. without or not subject to a particular feeling or sensation
22. appearance to the eye or mind
23. skilled in fluent, forceful and appropriate speech
24. make wrinkles in the face
26. personal disgrace, dishonor
29. added as a supplement
30. continues to irritate or cause bitter resentment
32. the face, usually with reference to shape, features, expression
33. to threaten, menace
34. disdainfully proud, snobbish, arrogant
35. wooden framework with holes for securing head and hands, used to expose offender to public derision
36. accustomed to, used to
37. having or showing acute mental discernment, shrewd

Down

1. involving one within another
2. exceptional or abnormal
4. without regret for wrongdoing
5. the quality or condition of being improper
7. being or demeanor
8. a formal discussion of a subject in speech or written talk, as a sermon
9. a hoop petticoat; or circles of hoops used to extend the petticoat
10. gloomy state of mind
17. eyes
18. stubbornness
20. spiteful; malignant
21. to become quiet, less active
25. hellish; diabolical, fiendish
27. boldly shameless
28. a shafted weapon with an axlike cutting blade, beak and spike
31. Roman Catholic

Scarlet Letter Vocab Ch 4-6A

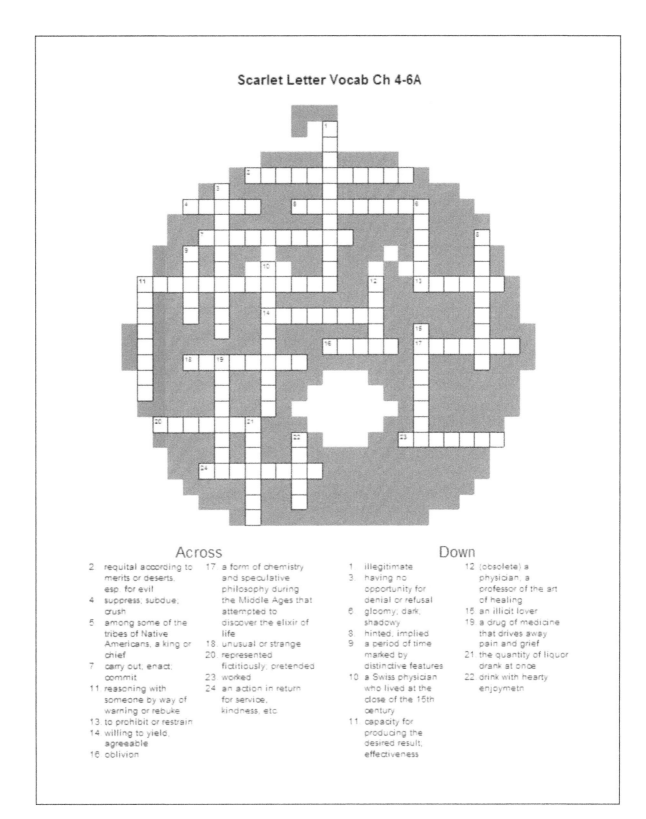

Across

2. requital according to merits or deserts, esp. for evil
4. suppress; subdue; crush
5. among some of the tribes of Native Americans, a king or chief
7. carry out; enact; commit
11. reasoning with someone by way of warning or rebuke
13. to prohibit or restrain
14. willing to yield, agreeable
16. oblivion
17. a form of chemistry and speculative philosophy during the Middle Ages that attempted to discover the elixir of life
18. unusual or strange
20. represented fictitiously; pretended
23. worked
24. an action in return for service, kindness, etc

Down

1. illegitimate
3. having no opportunity for denial or refusal
6. gloomy; dark; shadowy
8. hinted, implied
9. a period of time marked by distinctive features
10. a Swiss physician who lived at the close of the 15th century
11. capacity for producing the desired result; effectiveness
12. (obsolete) a physician; a professor of the art of healing
15. an illicit lover
19. a drug of medicine that drives away pain and grief
21. the quantity of liquor drank at once
22. drink with hearty enjoymetn

Scarlet Letter Vocab Ch 4-6A

Across

2. requital according to merits or deserts, esp. for evil
4. suppress; subdue; crush
5. among some of the tribes of Native Americans, a king or chief
7. carry out; enact; commit
11. reasoning with someone by way of warning or rebuke
13. to prohibit or restrain
14. willing to yield; agreeable
16. oblivion
17. a form of chemistry and speculative philosophy during the Middle Ages that attempted to discover the elixir of life
18. unusual or strange
20. represented fictitiously; pretended
23. worked
24. an action in return for service, kindness, etc.

Down

1. illegitimate
3. having no opportunity for denial or refusal
6. gloomy; dark; shadowy
8. hinted; implied
9. a period of time marked by distinctive features
10. a Swiss physician who lived at the close of the 15th century
11. capacity for producing the desired result; effectiveness
12. (obsolete) a physician, a professor of the art of healing
15. an illicit lover
19. a drug of medicine that drives away pain and grief
21. the quantity of liquor drank at once
22. drink with hearty enjoymetn

Scarlet Letter Vocab Ch 4-6B

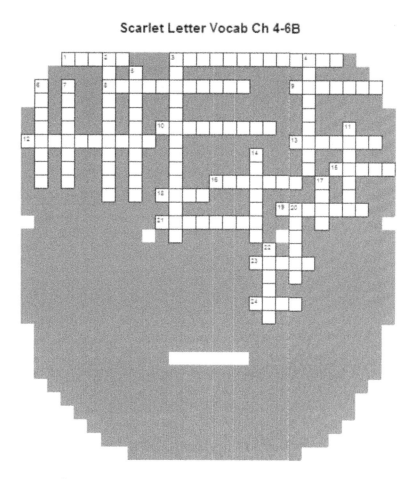

Across

1. general external appearance
3. the action of feeling or expressing sympathy for
8. a person or thing that originates something or serves as a model
9. austere; simple
10. compensation, as fees or tips, from employment
12. to take in and incorporate as one's own; absorb
13. to know; be aware of
15. black; dark
16. soiled; tarnished, stained
18. a neckpiece of lace gathered into deep, full, regular folds
19. to receive into the mind
21. of or pertaining to the common people
23. gruesome ; horrible , revolting
24. stately or splendid display; splendor

Down

2. being more than is sufficient or required; excessive
3. stubbornly perverse or rebellious; willfully disobedient
4. intended to entrap or beguile
5. characterized or ministering to indulgence in luxury
6. good luck charm
7. to be enough or adequate
11. a punishment undergone as penitence for sin
14. to make sore by rubbing; chafe
17. gladly; willingly
20. suggesting an unhealthy mental state or attitude; gloomy
22. to help or relieve in difficulty, need or distress

Scarlet Letter Vocab Ch 4-6B

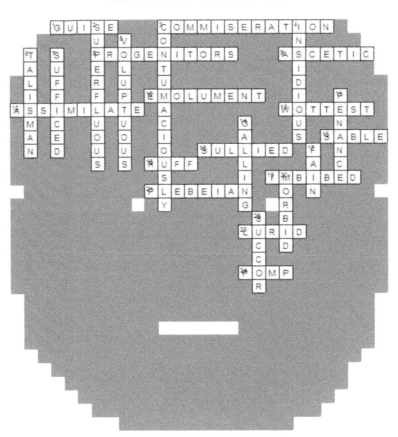

Across

1. general external appearance
3. the action of feeling or expressing sympathy for
8. a person or thing that originates something or serves as a model
9. austere, simple
10. compensation, as fees or tips, from employment
12. to take in and incorporate as one's own; absorb
13. to know, be aware of
15. black; dark
16. soiled; tarnished; stained
18. a neckpiece of lace gathered into deep, full, regular folds
19. to receive into the mind
21. of or pertaining to the common people
23. gruesome, horrible, revolting
24. stately or splendid display; splendor

Down

2. being more than is sufficient or required; excessive
3. stubbornly perverse or rebellious; willfully disobedient
4. intended to entrap or beguile
5. characterized or ministering to indulgence in luxury
6. good luck charm
7. to be enough or adequate
11. a punishment undergone as penitence for sin
14. to make sore by rubbing; chafe
17. gladly; willingly
20. suggesting an unhealthy mental state or attitude; gloomy
22. to help or relieve in difficulty, need or distress

Scarlet Letter Vocab Ch 4-6C

Across

3. displaying in a sporting manner
7. the act of using gestures in an excited manner
8. obtained
9. unbelief
13. peacefulness
14. saturated deeply
15. curses
17. to assert or affirm with confidence
18. whipping or lashing, esp. for punishment
19. a maze
20. a question; an inquiry

Down

1. not material
2. an elf, fairy, or goblin
4. subject to change or alteration
5. highly productive
6. not easily understood; mysterious
10. a sudden unpredictable change
11. an abrupt, exclamatory utterance
12. common people of society
16. to speak abusively

Scarlet Letter Vocab Ch 4-6C

Across

3. displaying in a sporting manner
7. the act of using gestures in an excited manner
8. obtained
9. unbelief
13. peacefulness
14. saturated deeply
15. curses
17. to assert or affirm with confidence
18. whipping or lashing, esp. for punishment
19. a maze
20. a question; an inquiry

Down

1. not material
2. an elf, fairy, or goblin
4. subject to change or alteration
5. highly productive
6. not easily understood; mysterious
10. a sudden unpredictable change
11. an abrupt exclamatory utterance
12. common people of society
16. to speak abusively

Scarlet Letter Vocab Ch 7-8A

Across

1. likeness ; resemblance
4. a deadly or virulent epidemic disease
5. to form like a bow, to arch; to vault
6. domineering; dictatorial
9. absurd ; ridiculous
11. to occupy a position at the flank or side
12. containing an occult meaning
13. leap or skip about in a sprightly manner
15. still existing
16. pale; faint or deficient in color
17. having its original purity
18. a door, gate, or entrance

Down

2. not planned beforehand
3. showing or suggesting ill health
6. belonging to a thing by its very nature
7. to drive or urge forward
8. any small boy or youngster
10. bold; not intimidated
14. a similarity between like features of two things
19. a book; esp a very heavy, large, or learned book

Scarlet Letter Vocab Ch 7-8A

Across

1. likeness ; resemblance
4. a deadly or virulent epidemic disease
5. to form like a bow, to arch; to vault
6. domineering; dictatorial
9. absurd ; ridiculous
11. to occupy a position at the flank or side
12. containing an occult meaning
13. leap or skip about in a sprightly manner
15. still existing
16. pale; faint or deficient in color
17. having its original purity
18. a door, gate, or entrance

Down

2. not planned beforehand
3. showing or suggesting ill health
6. belonging to a thing by its very nature
7. to drive or urge forward
8. any small boy or youngster
10. bold; not intimidated
14. a similarity between like features of two things
19. a book; esp. a very heavy, large, or learned book

Scarlet Letter Vocab Ch 7-8B

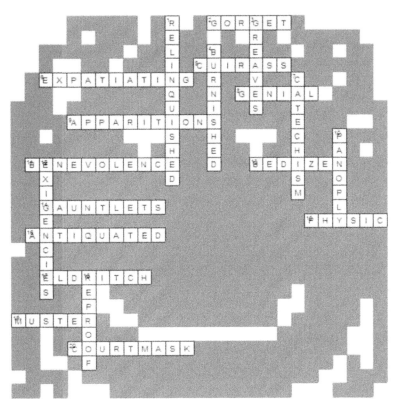

Across

2. a piece of armor for defending the neck or throat
5. a breast-plate; a piece of defensive armor
6. elaborating in discourse or writing
8. warmly and pleasantly cheerful
9. ghosts; specters
11. desire to do good to others
13. to dress or adorn gaudily or tastelessly
14. a large iron glove with fingers covered with small plates
15. the art or practice of healing medicine
16. old fashioned; obsolete
17. weird; eerie
19. to assemble troops, as for battle or inspection
20. masquerade party

Down

1. gave up; surrendered
3. armor for the legs; a sort of boots
4. polished
7. instruction by question and answer
10. a wide-ranging and impressive array or display
12. a state of urgency or emergency
18. criticism or correction

Scarlet Letter Vocab Ch 7-8B

Across

2. a piece of armor for defending the neck or throat
5. a breast-plate; a piece of defensive armor
6. elaborating in discourse or writing
8. warmly and pleasantly cheerful
9. ghosts; specters
11. desire to do good to others
13. to dress or adorn gaudily or tastelessly
14. a large iron glove with fingers covered with small plates
15. the art or practice of healing medicine
16. old fashioned; obsolete
17. weird, eerie
19. to assemble troops, as for battle or inspection
20. masquerade party

Down

1. gave up; surrendered
3. armor for the legs; a sort of boots
4. polished
7. instruction by question and answer
10. a wide-ranging and impressive array or display
12. a state of urgency or emergency
18. criticism or correction

146

Scarlet Letter Vocab Ch 7-8C

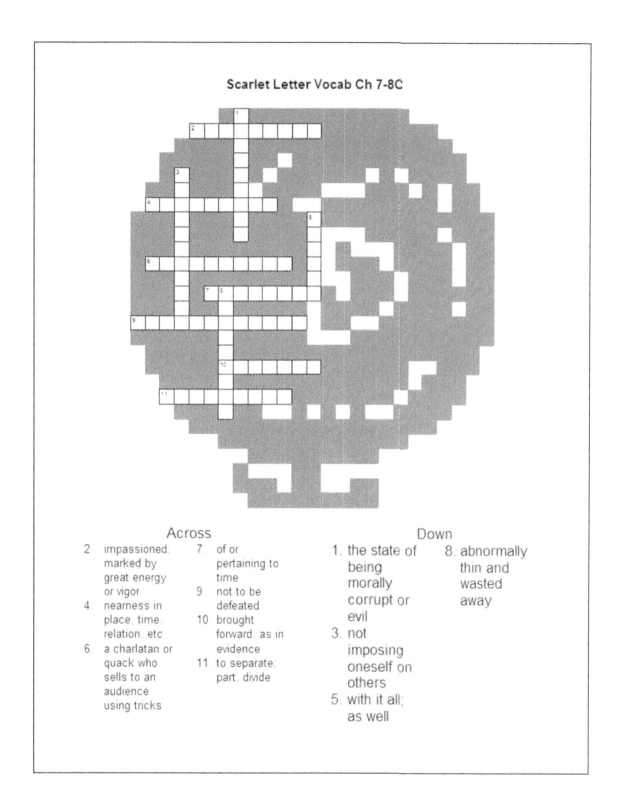

Across

2. impassioned; marked by great energy or vigor
4. nearness in place, time, relation, etc.
6. a charlatan or quack who sells to an audience using tricks
7. of or pertaining to time
9. not to be defeated
10. brought forward, as in evidence
11. to separate; part, divide

Down

1. the state of being morally corrupt or evil
3. not imposing oneself on others
5. with it all; as well
8. abnormally thin and wasted away

Scarlet Letter Vocab Ch 7-8C

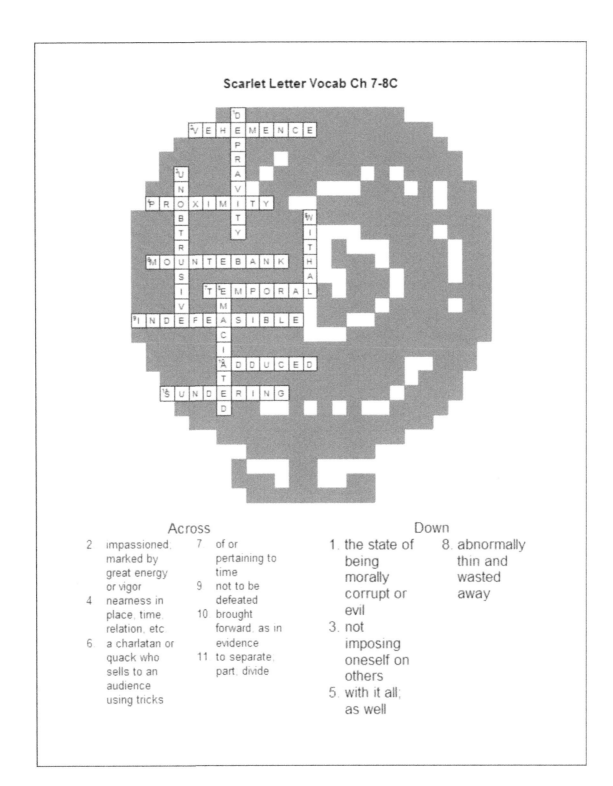

Across

2 impassioned, marked by great energy or vigor
4 nearness in place, time, relation, etc.
6 a charlatan or quack who sells to an audience using tricks
7 of or pertaining to time
9 not to be defeated
10 brought forward, as in evidence
11 to separate, part, divide

Down

1. the state of being morally corrupt or evil
3. not imposing oneself on others
5. with it all; as well
8. abnormally thin and wasted away

148

Scarlet Letter Vocab Ch 9-11A

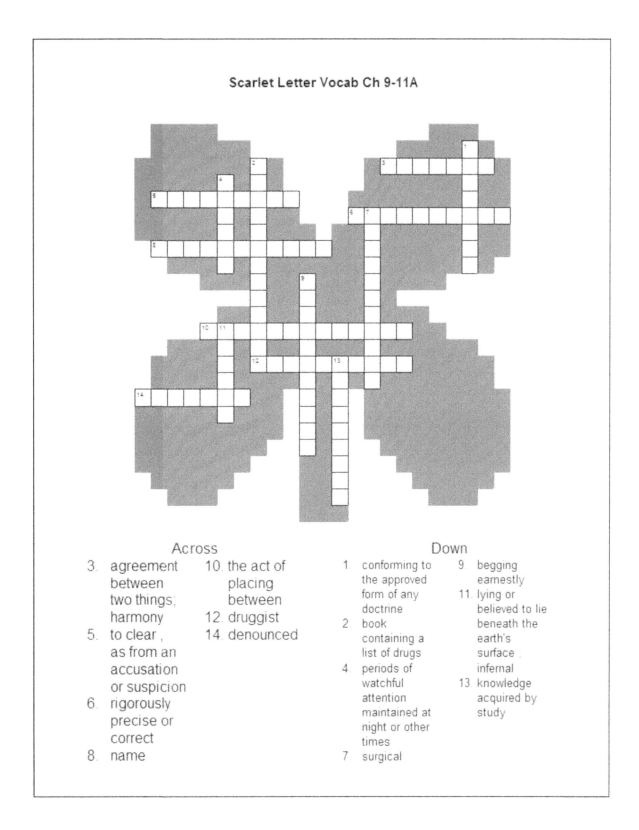

Across

3. agreement between two things; harmony
5. to clear, as from an accusation or suspicion
6. rigorously precise or correct
8. name
10. the act of placing between
12. druggist
14. denounced

Down

1. conforming to the approved form of any doctrine
2. book containing a list of drugs
4. periods of watchful attention maintained at night or other times
7. surgical
9. begging earnestly
11. lying or believed to lie beneath the earth's surface; infernal
13. knowledge acquired by study

Scarlet Letter Vocab Ch 9-11A

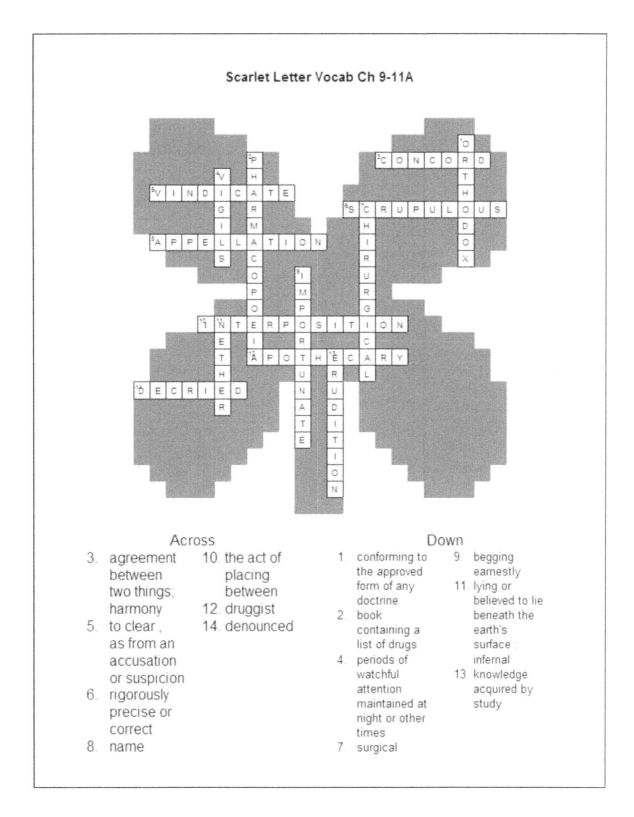

Across

3. agreement between two things; harmony
5. to clear, as from an accusation or suspicion
6. rigorously precise or correct
8. name
10. the act of placing between
12. druggist
14. denounced

Down

1. conforming to the approved form of any doctrine
2. book containing a list of drugs
4. periods of watchful attention maintained at night or other times
7. surgical
9. begging earnestly
11. lying or believed to lie beneath the earth's surface; infernal
13. knowledge acquired by study

Scarlet Letter Vocab Ch 9-11B

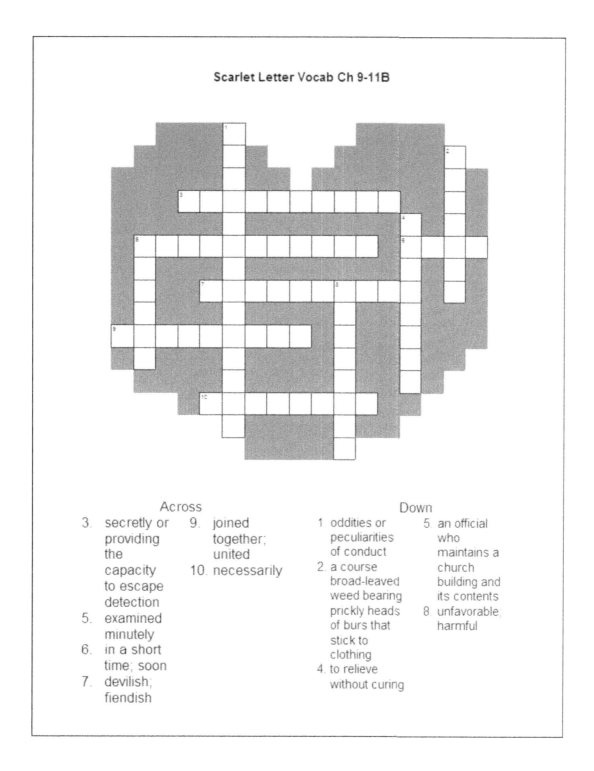

Across

3. secretly or providing the capacity to escape detection
5. examined minutely
6. in a short time; soon
7. devilish; fiendish
9. joined together; united
10. necessarily

Down

1. oddities or peculiarities of conduct
2. a course broad-leaved weed bearing prickly heads of burs that stick to clothing
4. to relieve without curing
5. an official who maintains a church building and its contents
8. unfavorable; harmful

Scarlet Letter Vocab Ch 9-11B

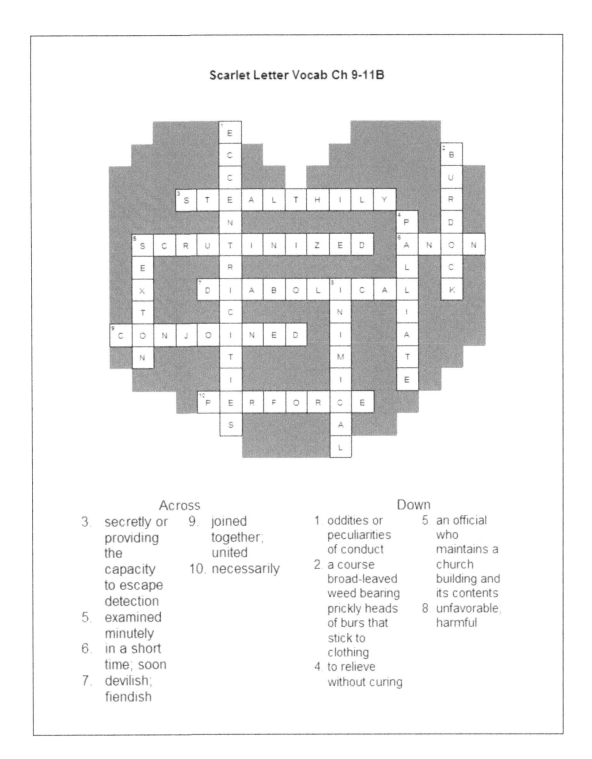

Across

3. secretly or providing the capacity to escape detection
5. examined minutely
6. in a short time; soon
7. devilish; fiendish
9. joined together; united
10. necessarily

Down

1. oddities or peculiarities of conduct
2. a course broad-leaved weed bearing prickly heads of burs that stick to clothing
4. to relieve without curing
5. an official who maintains a church building and its contents
8. unfavorable; harmful

Scarlet Letter Vocab Ch 9-11C

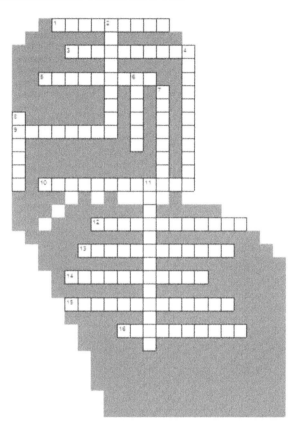

Across

1. a natural repugnance; aversion
3. detestable; loathsome
5. not friendly
9. hard to understand
10. crafty schemes or maneuvers; intrigues
12. made heavenly or celestial
13. not giving a false or misleading appearance to
14. causing sleep
15. feelings that something bad is going to happen
16. put before a person for acceptance

Down

2. cause an increase in number or amount
4. capable of having the desired result or effect
6. present but not visible; dormant
7. up to this time
8. stopped short and stubbornly refused to go on
11. given to examining one's own thoughts and emotions

Scarlet Letter Vocab Ch 9-11C

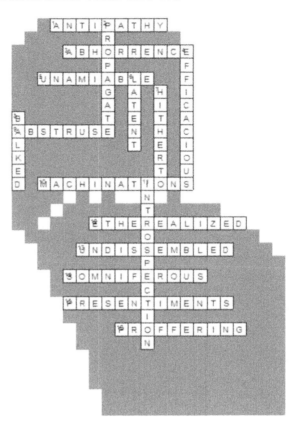

Across

1. a natural repugnance; aversion
3. detestable; loathsome
5. not friendly
9. hard to understand
10. crafty schemes or maneuvers; intrigues
12. made heavenly or celestial
13. not giving a false or misleading appearance to
14. causing sleep
15. feelings that something bad is going to happen
16. put before a person for acceptance

Down

2. cause an increase in number or amount
4. capable of having the desired result or effect
6. present but not visible; dormant
7. up to this time
8. stopped short and stubbornly refused to go on
11. given to examining one's own thoughts and emotions

Scarlet Letter Vocab Ch 12A

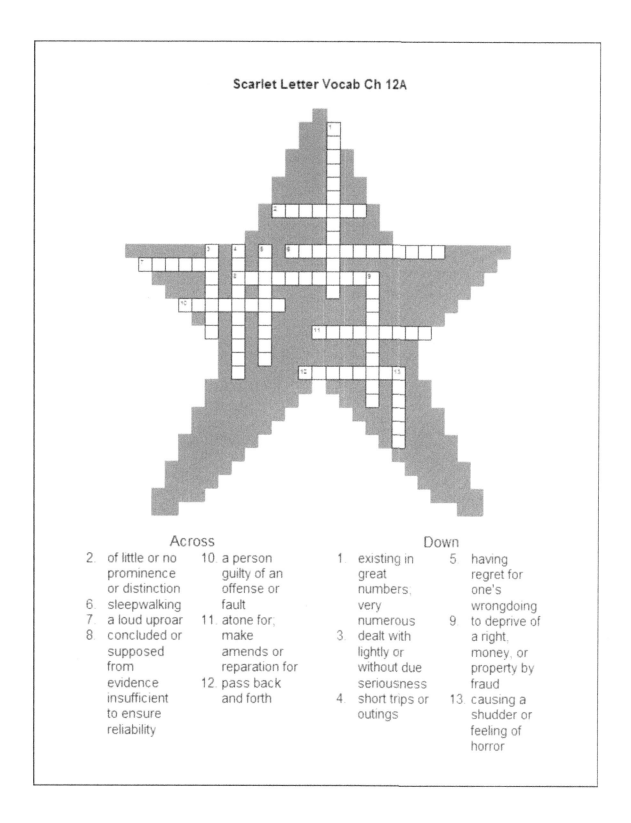

Across

2. of little or no prominence or distinction
6. sleepwalking
7. a loud uproar
8. concluded or supposed from evidence insufficient to ensure reliability
10. a person guilty of an offense or fault
11. atone for; make amends or reparation for
12. pass back and forth

Down

1. existing in great numbers; very numerous
3. dealt with lightly or without due seriousness
4. short trips or outings
5. having regret for one's wrongdoing
9. to deprive of a right, money, or property by fraud
13. causing a shudder or feeling of horror

The Scarlet Letter

Scarlet Letter Vocab Ch 12A

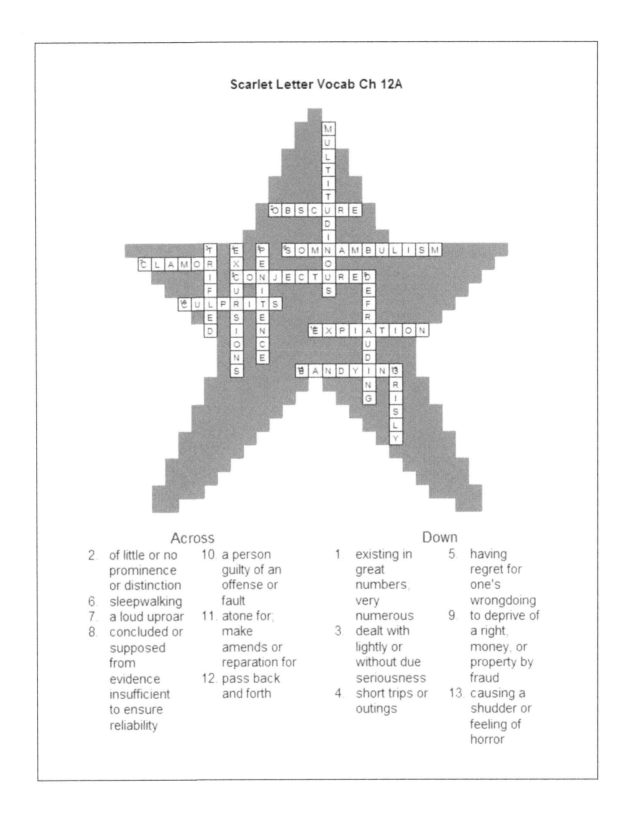

Across

2. of little or no prominence or distinction
6. sleepwalking
7. a loud uproar
8. concluded or supposed from evidence insufficient to ensure reliability
10. a person guilty of an offense or fault
11. atone for; make amends or reparation for
12. pass back and forth

Down

1. existing in great numbers; very numerous
3. dealt with lightly or without due seriousness
4. short trips or outings
5. having regret for one's wrongdoing
9. to deprive of a right, money, or property by fraud
13. causing a shudder or feeling of horror

156

Scarlet Letter Vocab Ch 12B

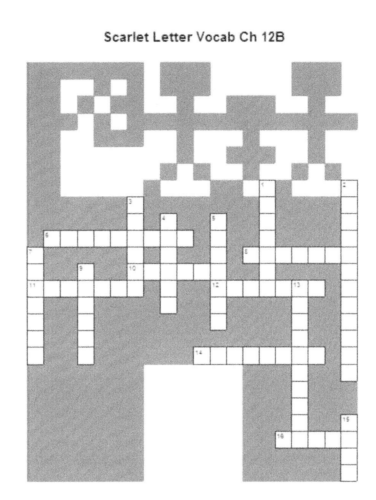

Across

6. belonging to or seen in a vision
8. no longer in existence
10. a violent and noisy commotion
11. inflammation of a mucous membrane, esp. of the respiratory tract
12. selfishness; self-centeredness
14. a body, object, etc. that gives light; an important person
16. crookedly

Down

1. a rushing, violent, or abundant stream of anything
2. incapable of being disentangled, undone, or loosed
3. highest point
4. sternly; harshly
5. an indication or omen of something about to happen
7. ridicule ; derision
9. increase in extent
13. grossly or obscenely abusive
15. away from the expected or proper direction; amiss

Scarlet Letter Vocab Ch 12B

Across

6. belonging to or seen in a vision
8. no longer in existence
10. a violent and noisy commotion
11. inflammation of a mucous membrane, esp. of the respiratory tract
12. selfishness; self-centeredness
14. a body, object, etc. that gives light; an important person
16. crookedly

Down

1. a rushing, violent, or abundant stream of anything
2. incapable of being disentangled, undone, or loosed
3. highest point
4. sternly; harshly
5. an indication or omen of something about to happen
7. ridicule ; derision
9. increase in extent
13. grossly or obscenely abusive
15. away from the expected or proper direction; amiss

Scarlet Letter Vocab Ch 13-14

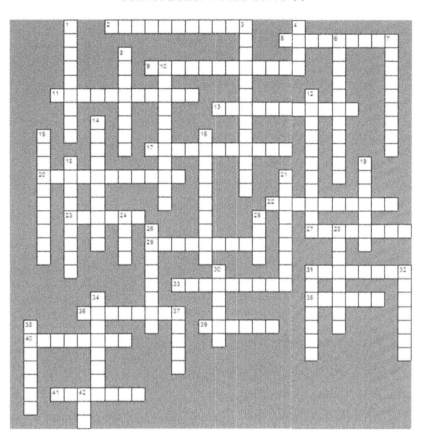

Across

2. annoying; irritating
5. extravagantly fanciful; lavish
9. chance; doubt; uncertainty
11. broken; incomplete
13. set with some mark of disgrace or infamy
17. the contemplation or consideration of some subject
20. nearness in time or place
22. ridiculing; mocking
23. of kindly disposition; gracious
27. lie or crawl with the face downward and the body prostrate
29. something that flows out
31. stirred up
33. outward aspect or appearance
35. to obtain by force, threat, intimidation, or abuse of authority
36. tyrannical; oppressive
39. a command; directive
40. to seize and hold by force or without legal right
41. shockingly frightful or dreadful ; horrible

Down

1. bestowed as a gift, favor or honor
3. meaning; import; sense
4. a person or thing that ruins or spoils
6. submit or comply without protest
7. to force, compel, or oblige
8. tranquility; peacefulness
10. set free
12. talking; conversing
14. conspicuous
15. a natural tendency or inclination
16. prosperous; fortunate
18. have a feeling of future evil
19. obstructed; hindered
21. a cliff with a vertical or overhanging face
24. insulting remark
25. reward
26. determined; firmly set in purpose
28. to anticipate and prevent
30. humiliated; degraded
31. to take vengeance on
32. to see; recognize
34. dangerous
37. a deep gap or break
38. a purpose or intention
42. suited to the purpose or occasion

Scarlet Letter Vocab Ch 13-14

Across

2. annoying; irritating
5. extravagantly fanciful; lavish
9. chance; doubt; uncertainty
11. broken; incomplete
13. set with some mark of disgrace or infamy
17. the contemplation or consideration of some subject
20. nearness in time or place
22. ridiculing; mocking
23. of kindly disposition; gracious
27. lie or crawl with the face downward and the body prostrate
29. something that flows out
31. stirred up
33. outward aspect or appearance
35. to obtain by force, threat, intimidation, or abuse of authority
36. tyrannical; oppressive
39. a command; directive
40. to seize and hold by force or without legal right
41. shockingly frightful or dreadful; horrible

Down

1. bestowed as a gift, favor or honor
3. meaning; import; sense
4. a person or thing that ruins or spoils
6. submit or comply without protest
7. to force, compel, or oblige
8. tranquility; peacefulness
10. set free
12. talking; conversing
14. conspicuous
15. a natural tendency or inclination
16. prosperous; fortunate
18. have a feeling of future evil
19. obstructed; hindered
21. a cliff with a vertical or overhanging face
24. insulting remark
25. reward
26. determined; firmly set in purpose
28. to anticipate and prevent
30. humiliated; degraded
31. to take vengeance on
32. to see, recognize
34. dangerous
37. a deep gap or break
38. a purpose or intention
42. suited to the purpose or occasion

Scarlet Letter Vocab Ch 15-16A

Across

1. to give, feel in return
3. erratic
6. injurious to health
8. of or pertaining to marriage
9. disobedience
13. unusually advanced or mature in mental development
14. to become wrecked; fail utterly
18. deteriorated or ruined
19. greenness
20. portending evil or harm

Down

2. inconsistent
4. showing sudden irritation
5. not able to be felt
7. to take great pleasure in
10. withered
11. sharpness
12. a primer formerly used in teaching children to read
15. skill using the hands
16. instances of misbehaviors
17. diligent; persevering

Scarlet Letter Vocab Ch 15-16A

Across

1. to give, feel in return
3. erratic
6. injurious to health
8. of or pertaining to marriage
9. disobedience
13. unusually advanced or mature in mental development
14. to become wrecked; fail utterly
18. deteriorated or ruined
19. greenness
20. portending evil or harm

Down

2. inconsistent
4. showing sudden irritation
5. not able to be felt
7. to take great pleasure in
10. withered
11. sharpness
12. a primer formerly used in teaching children to read
15. skill using the hands
16. instances of misbehaviors
17. diligent, persevering

Scarlet Letter Vocab Ch 15-16B

Across

1. before
3. of or pertaining to the first age or ages
5. doing good or causing good
8. existing in one from birth
9. open or unqualified contempt
10. harshness or sharpness of tone
12. about to happen
15. pictured, imagined
17. sharply stinging or bitter
19. intentionally kept concealed

Down

2. to be animated; witty; sparkling
3. thoughtfulness or sadness
4. animated; spirited
6. the extreme limit
7. a disease characterized by tumors in the glands of the neck, under the chin, in the armpits, etc.
11. a puzzling occurrence or situation
13. to what place; where
14. charged with a fault
16. small whirlpools
18. a small, usually wooded valley

Scarlet Letter Vocab Ch 15-16B

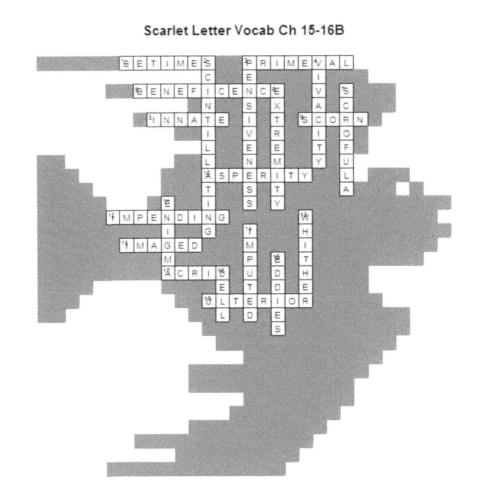

Across

1. before
3. of or pertaining to the first age or ages
5. doing good or causing good
8. existing in one from birth
9. open or unqualified contempt
10. harshness or sharpness of tone
12. about to happen
15. pictured, imagined
17. sharply stinging or bitter
19. intentionally kept concealed

Down

2. to be animated; witty; sparkling
3. thoughtfulness or sadness
4. animated; spirited
6. the extreme limit
7. a disease characterized by tumors in the glands of the neck, under the chin, in the armpits, etc.
11. a puzzling occurrence or situation
13. to what place; where
14. charged with a fault
16. small whirlpools
18. a small, usually wooded valley

Scarlet Letter Vocab Ch 15-16C

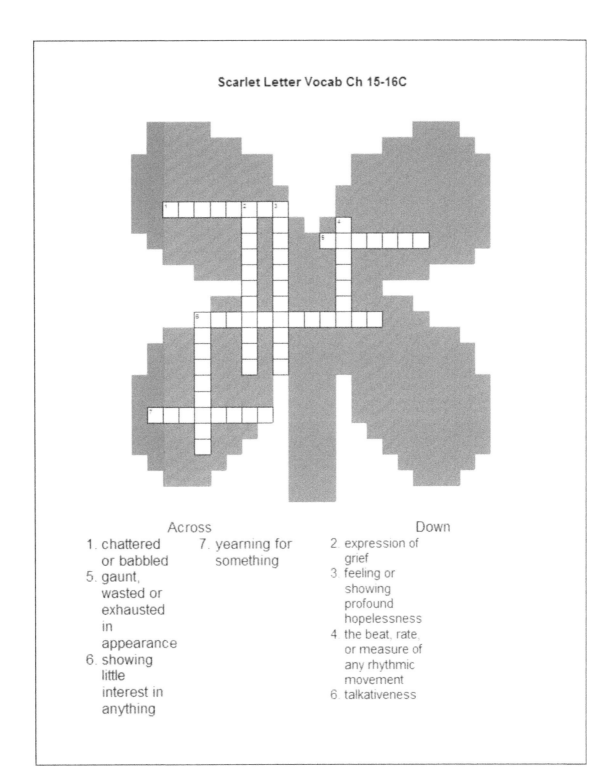

Across

1. chattered or babbled
5. gaunt, wasted or exhausted in appearance
6. showing little interest in anything
7. yearning for something

Down

2. expression of grief
3. feeling or showing profound hopelessness
4. the beat, rate, or measure of any rhythmic movement
6. talkativeness

Scarlet Letter Vocab Ch 15-16C

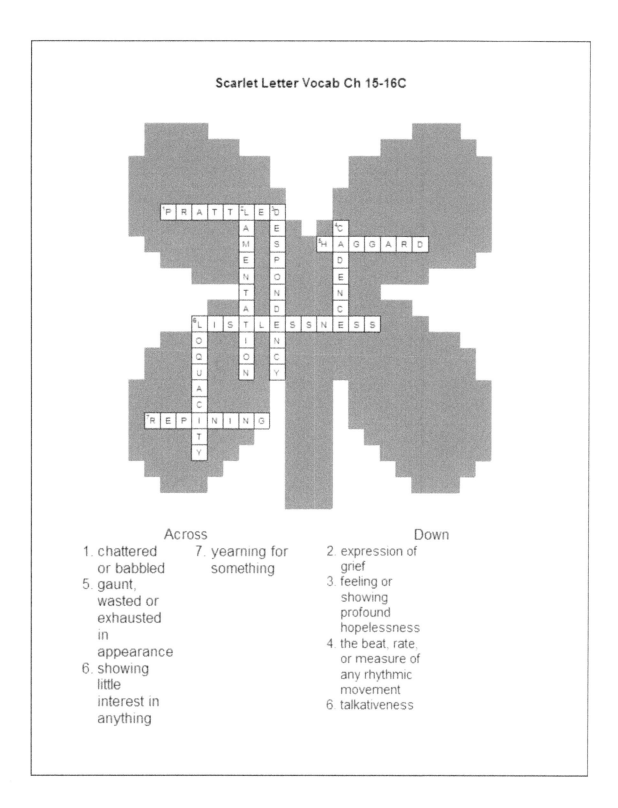

Across

1. chattered or babbled
5. gaunt, wasted or exhausted in appearance
6. showing little interest in anything
7. yearning for something

Down

2. expression of grief
3. feeling or showing profound hopelessness
4. the beat, rate, or measure of any rhythmic movement
6. talkativeness

Scarlet Letter Vocab Ch 17-19A

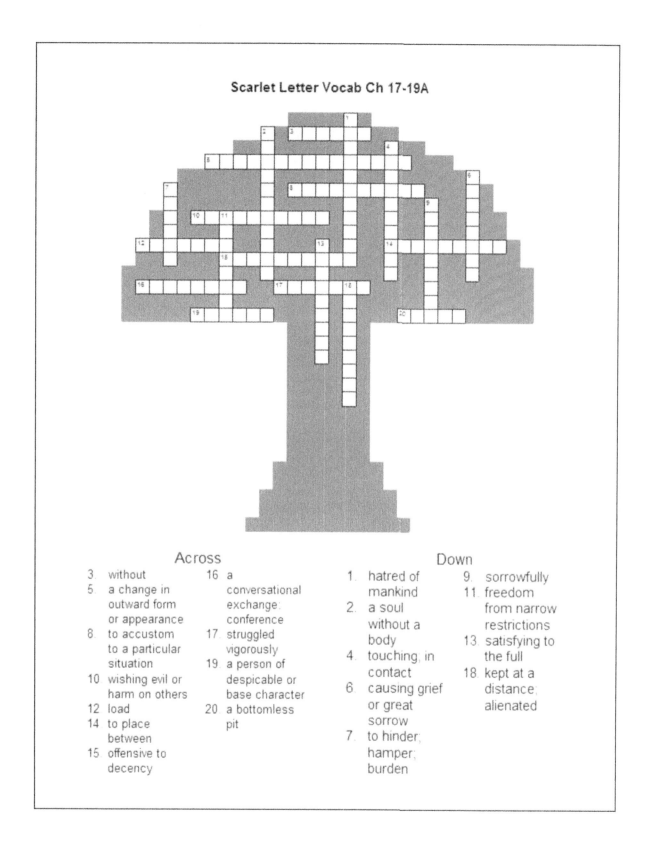

Across

3. without
5. a change in outward form or appearance
8. to accustom to a particular situation
10. wishing evil or harm on others
12. load
14. to place between
15. offensive to decency
16. a conversational exchange; conference
17. struggled vigorously
19. a person of despicable or base character
20. a bottomless pit

Down

1. hatred of mankind
2. a soul without a body
4. touching, in contact
6. causing grief or great sorrow
7. to hinder; hamper; burden
9. sorrowfully
11. freedom from narrow restrictions
13. satisfying to the full
18. kept at a distance; alienated

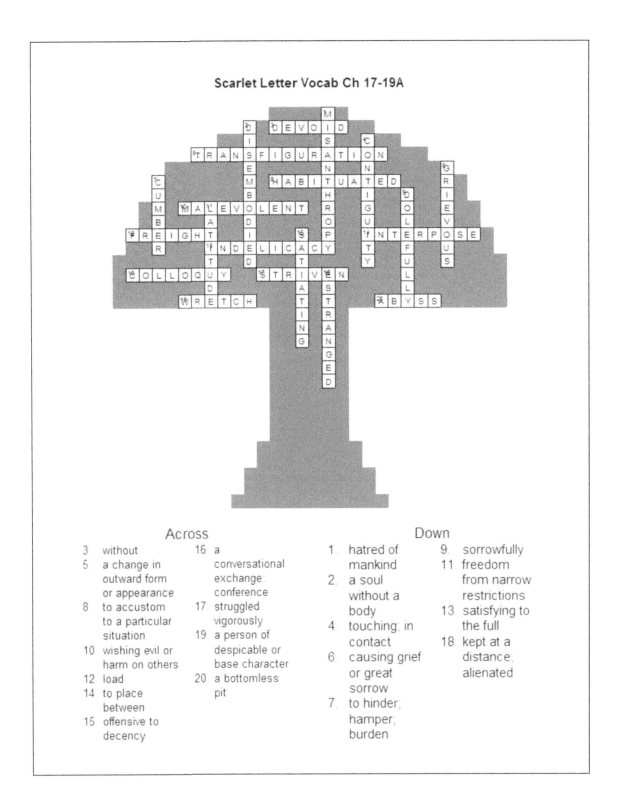

Scarlet Letter Vocab Ch 17-19A

Across

3. without
5. a change in outward form or appearance
8. to accustom to a particular situation
10. wishing evil or harm on others
12. load
14. to place between
15. offensive to decency
16. a conversational exchange; conference
17. struggled vigorously
19. a person of despicable or base character
20. a bottomless pit

Down

1. hatred of mankind
2. a soul without a body
4. touching; in contact
6. causing grief or great sorrow
7. to hinder; hamper; burden
9. sorrowfully
11. freedom from narrow restrictions
13. satisfying to the full
18. kept at a distance; alienated

Scarlet Letter Vocab Ch 17-19B

Across

1. a stain or reproach on one's reputation
2. unable to be avoided
8. the combination of mental and emotional traits of a person
10. a nymph of the woods
11. atoning for; making amends for
12. drawing out of shape
14. earnest requests; pleas
15. softened in feeling or temper; pacified; appeased
16. changing from one nature or condition to another
19. a system of writing consisting of pictographs
21. toughened or hardened by use or exposure
24. inhabitants; residents
26. invigorating
27. corrupted
28. visually charming or quaint

Down

1. comfort
3. to make or try to make seem less serious by offering excuses
4. not to be revoked or recalled
5. restrained
6. attentive to the smallest detail
7. wearing away by irritation
8. provoking expectation, interest, or desire
9. decorate
13. a class of lesser mythological deities inhabiting the seas, rivers, trees, or mountains
17. make or use gestures in an animated or excited manner
18. sinned
20. easily angered
22. brought under control; mastered
23. a fortress
25. intense; acute

Scarlet Letter Vocab Ch 17-19B

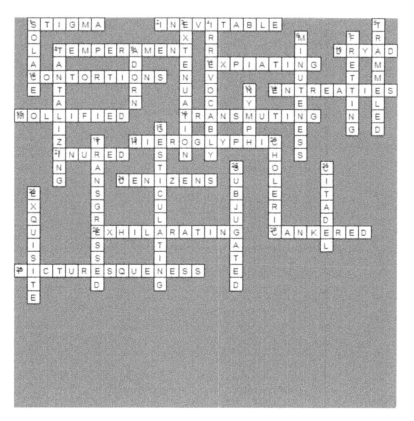

Across

1 a stain or reproach on one's reputation
2 unable to be avoided
8 the combination of mental and emotional traits of a person
10 a nymph of the woods
11 atoning for; making amends for
12 drawing out of shape
14 earnest requests, pleas
15 softened in feeling or temper, pacified, appeased
16 changing from one nature or condition to another
19 a system of writing consisting of pictographs
21 toughened or hardened by use or exposure
24 inhabitants, residents
26 invigorating
27 corrupted
28 visually charming or quaint

Down

1 comfort
3 to make or try to make seem less serious by offering excuses
4 not to be revoked or recalled
5 restrained
6 attentive to the smallest detail
7 wearing away by irritation
8 provoking expectation, interest, or desire
9 decorate
13 a class of lesser mythological deities inhabiting the seas, rivers, trees, or mountains
17 make or use gestures in an animated or excited manner
18 sinned
20 easily angered
22 brought under control; mastered
23 a fortress
25 intense; acute

Scarlet Letter Vocab Ch 20-24A

Across

4. brief, forceful and meaningful in expression
5. regular change or succession of one state or thing to another
8. puddles
9. subject to change

Down

1. speak irreverently of God
2. not to be disputed or contested
3. a sequence of rulers from the same family or group
6. ancient times
7. stimulated to action
10. rude, uncivil, boorish

Scarlet Letter Vocab Ch 20-24A

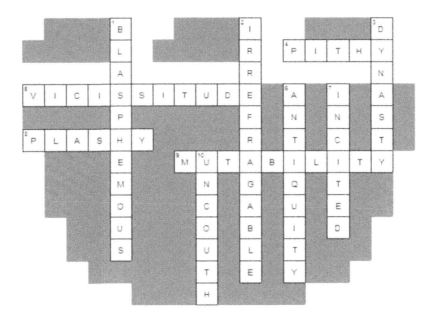

Across

4. brief, forceful and meaningful in expression
5. regular change or succession of one state or thing to another
8. puddles
9. subject to change

Down

1. speak irreverently of God
2. not to be disputed or contested
3. a sequence of rulers from the same family or group
6. ancient times
7. stimulated to action
10. rude, uncivil, boorish

Scarlet Letter Vocab Ch 20-24B

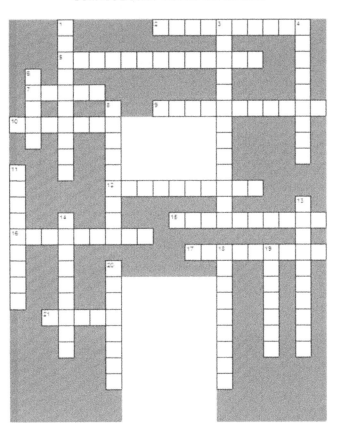

Across

2. to pay or give compensation for
5. showing enthusiasm, excitement, or liveliness
7. medicine used as a laxative
9. continuing or enduring forever
10. a musician
12. made holy
15. lasting only a short time
16. understand
17. deceitfulness
21. irritated, annoyed

Down

1. something that is remarkable or extraordinary
3. state of being seen by the eye
4. commendable
6. triangular shape enclosed by or masking the end of a roof that slopes downward
8. tending to come in without permission
11. searched thoroughly and vigorously
13. being without cause or justification
14. a chief fiend; Satan
18. a person possessing great power, such as a ruler or monarch
19. a stimulating medicine
20. made; caused to be

Scarlet Letter Vocab Ch 20-24B

Across

2. to pay or give compensation for
5. showing enthusiasm, excitement, or liveliness
7. medicine used as a laxative
9. continuing or enduring forever
10. a musician
12. made holy
15. lasting only a short time
16. understand
17. deceitfulness
21. irritated; annoyed

Down

1. something that is remarkable or extraordinary
3. state of being seen by the eye
4. commendable
6. triangular shape enclosed by or masking the end of a roof that slopes downward
8. tending to come in without permission
11. searched thoroughly and vigorously
13. being without cause or justification
14. a chief fiend; Satan
18. a person possessing great power, such as a ruler or monarch
19. a stimulating medicine
20. made; caused to be

Scarlet Letter Vocab Ch 20-24C

Across

5. an unfavorable or critical comment
7. having a bad reputation ; dishonorable
9. buffoon; clown
11. made holy
13. having a disposition to impose oneself or one's opinions on others
14. bold, reckless outlaws
16. proper conduct

Down

1. sudden, alarming amazement or dread that results in confusion
2. stormy; turbulent
3. reverence for God
4. acts of robbery and violence
6. kept down or suppressed
8. working or acting merely for money
10. be on top or above
12. strong alcoholic liquor
15. disease caused by lack of vitamin C

Scarlet Letter Vocab Ch 20-24C

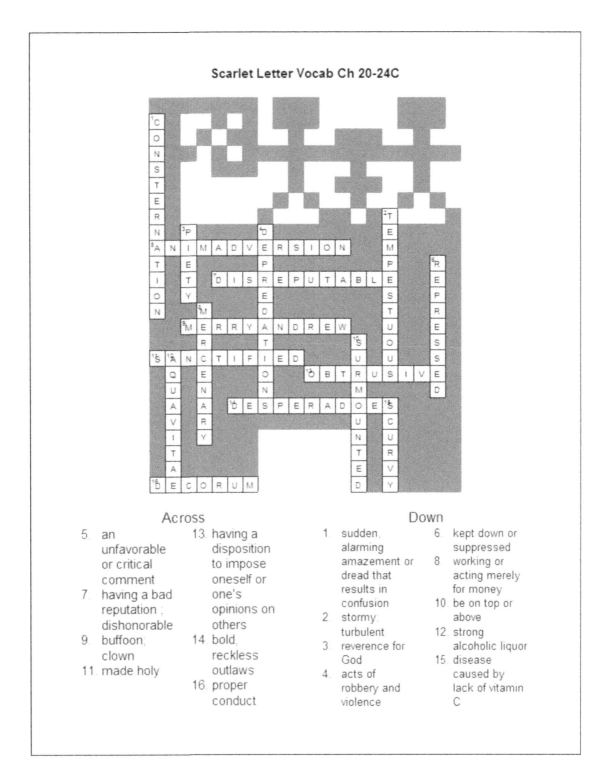

Across

5. an unfavorable or critical comment
7. having a bad reputation ; dishonorable
9. buffoon, clown
11. made holy
13. having a disposition to impose oneself or one's opinions on others
14. bold, reckless outlaws
16. proper conduct

Down

1. sudden, alarming amazement or dread that results in confusion
2. stormy, turbulent
3. reverence for God
4. acts of robbery and violence
6. kept down or suppressed
8. working or acting merely for money
10. be on top or above
12. strong alcoholic liquor
15. disease caused by lack of vitamin C

Scarlet Letter Vocab Ch 20-24D

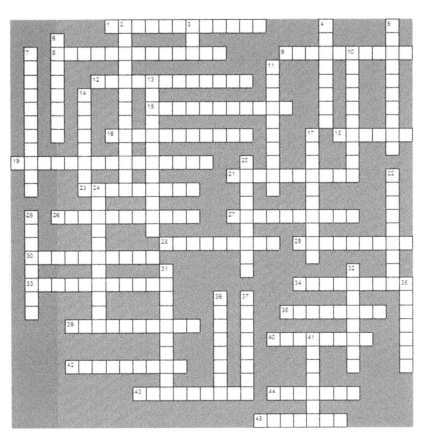

Across

1. deified; glorified
8. incapable of being tired out
9. bewilderment
12. completeness
15. a harmonious combination of elements
16. one who practices divination through invocation of the dead
18. rest; tranquility
19. military order during the Crusades
21. touching; in contact
23. indifferent to moral restraints; immoral
26. directed outward from the center
27. disposed of property in a will
28. great quantity
29. uncompromised honesty; soundness of moral character
30. any instrument or device for a particular purpose or use
33. obstacles
34. an ornament or support to the breast; worn by females
38. associates; equals
39. thought of apart from concrete reality
40. something bitter, grievous or extremely unpleasant
42. pirate
43. lacking vigor or vitality
44. one who listens
45. affected an angry expression

Down

2. expressing sorrow or melancholy
3. a sphere or globe
4. longing, aiming, or seeking ambitiously
5. too deep to understand
6. a medieval poet, singer, and musician
7. incentives
10. the property, funds, etc. with which a person or institution is furnished
11. characterized by joking
13. not restrained by morals; unprincipled
14. unusual
17. moving in wave-like motion
20. future generations
22. mental and emotional strength
24. indicated or made known directly
25. shameless boldness
31. a shield or shield-like surface on which a coat of arms is depicted
32. extremely hungry
35. sorrow for wrongdoing
36. brisk; active
37. savagely fierce or cruel
41. inclined to or disposed to war

177

Scarlet Letter Vocab Ch 20-24D

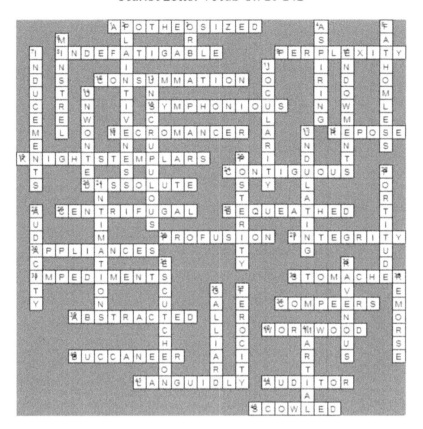

Across

1. deified, glorified
8. incapable of being tired out
9. bewilderment
12. completeness
15. a harmonious combination of elements
16. one who practices divination through invocation of the dead
18. rest, tranquility
19. military order during the Crusades
21. touching, in contact
23. indifferent to moral restraints, immoral
26. directed outward from the center
27. disposed of property in a will
28. great quantity
29. uncompromised honesty, soundness of moral character
30. any instrument or device for a particular purpose or use
33. obstacles
34. an ornament or support to the breast, worn by females
38. associates, equals
39. thought of apart from concrete reality
40. something bitter, grievous or extremely unpleasant
42. pirate
43. lacking vigor or vitality
44. one who listens
45. affected an angry expression

Down

2. expressing sorrow or melancholy
3. a sphere or globe
4. longing, aiming, or seeking ambitiously
5. too deep to understand
6. a medieval poet, singer, and musician
7. incentives
10. the property, funds, etc. with which a person or institution is furnished
11. characterized by joking
13. not restrained by morals; unprincipled
14. unusual
17. moving in wave-like motion
20. future generations
22. mental and emotional strength
24. indicated or made known directly
25. shameless boldness
31. a shield or shield-like surface on which a coat of arms is depicted
32. extremely hungry
35. sorrow for wrongdoing
36. brisk; active
37. savagely fierce or cruel
41. inclined to or disposed to war

178

Scarlet Letter Vocab Ch 20-24E

Across

2. brilliantly clear
5. noonday
6. filled with horror and fear
8. nearness
11. moral or ethical consideration that constrains one's behavior
13. rude; unmannerly
14. those who deliver authoritative and influential pronouncements
15. priest or cleric

Down

1. seriousness
3. trifling or worthless
4. lack of energy
7. pertaining to a coat of arms
9. something of little value, importance, or consequence
10. pity
12. integrity and uprightness; honesty

Scarlet Letter Vocab Ch 20-24E

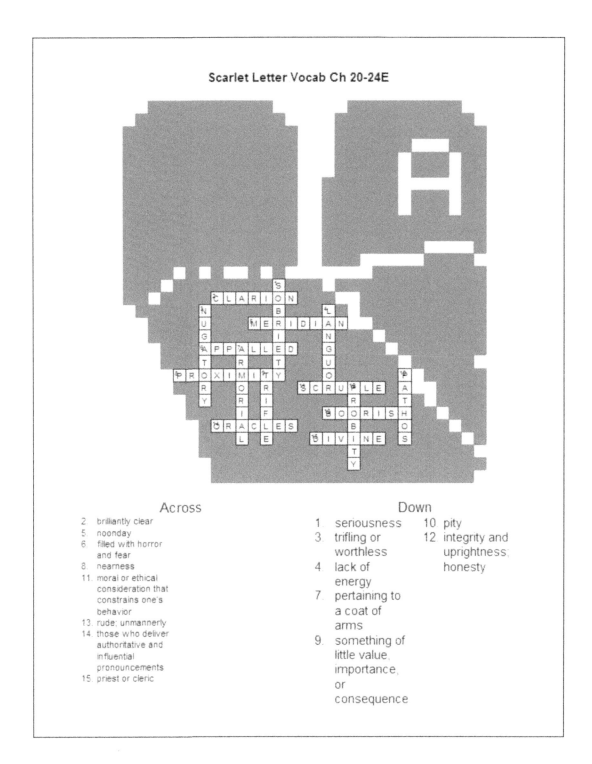

Across

2. brilliantly clear
5. noonday
6. filled with horror and fear
8. nearness
11. moral or ethical consideration that constrains one's behavior
13. rude; unmannerly
14. those who deliver authoritative and influential pronouncements
15. priest or cleric

Down

1. seriousness
3. trifling or worthless
4. lack of energy
7. pertaining to a coat of arms
9. something of little value, importance, or consequence
10. pity
12. integrity and uprightness; honesty

SELECTED BIBLIOGRAPHY

Biographical Material

Hawthorne, Julian. Hawthorne and His Circle. 1903.

_____. Nathaniel Hawthorne and His Wife. 1884.

http://www.eldritchpress.org/nh/nhahw.html. 2005.

http://www.uwm.edu/Library/special/exhibits/clastext/clspg143.htm. 2005.

http://en.wikipedia.org/wiki/Nathaniel_Hawthorne.htm. 2005.

Dictionaries

Slater, Rosalie J. Noah Webster's 1828 American Dictionary of the English
    Language. San Francisco:Foundation for American Christian
    Education, 1967 & 1995

Webster's Third International Dictionary .Springfield, MA: G & C.
    Merriam Co., 1963.

Webster's Universal College Dictionary . New York:Gramercy Books,
    1997.